WHY BELIEVE?

EXPLORING
THE HONEST
QUESTIONS
OF SEEKERS

This Billy Graham Library Selection special edition is
published by the Billy Graham Evangelistic Association
with permission from Tyndale House Publishers.

WHY BE

EXPLORING THE HONEST

TYNDALE HOUSE PUBLISHERS, INC.

GREG LAURIE

LIEVE?

QUESTIONS OF SEEKERS

WHEATON, ILLINOIS

Why Believe? Exploring the Honest Questions of Seekers

Copyright © 1995 by Greg Laurie. All rights reserved.

Designed by Dean H. Renninger

Edited by Susan Taylor

Published in 1995 as *Life. Any Questions?* by Word, Inc.

First Tyndale printing 2002, BGEA special edition printing 2003

Scripture quotations are taken from the New King James Version. Copyright © 1979, 1980, 1982 by Thomas Nelson, Inc. Used by permission. All rights reserved.

Library of Congress Cataloging-in-Publication Data

Laurie, Greg.
  [Life, any questions?]
  Why believe? : exploring the honest questions of seekers / Greg Laurie.
     p. cm.
Originally published: Life, any questions? Dallas : Word Pub., c1995.
Includes bibliographical references.
  ISBN 1-59328-001-7
  Previous ISBN 0-8423-5581-2
  1. Apologetics.   2. Spiritual life—Christianity.   3. United States—Religion—1960-
I. Title.
  BT1103 .L38 2002
  230—dc21   2001001990

Printed in the United States of America

A **Billy Graham Library Selection** designates materials that are appropriate to a well-rounded collection of quality Christian literature, including both classic and contemporary reading and reference materials.

CONTENTS

ACKNOWLEDGMENTS

Special thanks to Joseph Farah for his superb editing skills, Mark Ferjulian for his hard work and effort to bring this book to life, and to my staff at Harvest for helping me to bring this life-changing message to people around the world. I want to especially thank Ron Beers for having the vision to bring this book to many who need to read its message. Special thanks to my wife, Cathe, not only for being the perfect helpmeet but also for being a great sounding board for my ideas.

INTRODUCTION

I was born in 1952. That makes me a baby boomer.
The fifties—what a time to be alive! It all began so innocently.
James Dean was a movie star, and so was Marilyn Monroe.
John Kennedy was a senator, and Ike was president.
Ernest Hemingway was in his prime.
Elvis was king.

You could buy a handful of candy for a penny, and for twenty-five cents you could get a burger complete with the trimmings.

I spent a good deal of my childhood in southern California and remember watching *I Love Lucy* and *Leave It to Beaver* on black-and-white television. But life at our house was not like it was over at "the Beav's."

I came from a broken home, which often resulted in my being carted off to different parts of the country on short notice to live in various faraway places including New Jersey and Hawaii. I got used to the term "new kid," and because I was forced into being a loner because of the many moves we made, I was lonely much of the time; and because I had an artistic streak, I retreated into my private world of cartooning. In fact, growing up, it was my dream to one day become a professional cartoonist.

My dad was no Ward Cleaver. I was raised in a very adult world that was disillusioning. I quickly tired of the alcoholic haze that seemed to hover over my home life. I saw alcohol as symptomatic of the times and at an early age determined that there must be more to life than what I had seen so far.

I had a hard time growing up; in fact, I grew up too soon even in the age of innocence known as the fifties.

Then one day shots cracked the air in Dallas, and as bullets ripped through the body of President John F. Kennedy, the age of innocence came brutally to an end for me and my generation. No more illusions that life would ever be like it was depicted on TV—always a happy ending.

Other icons of our generation were checking out ahead of schedule too: James Dean was killed in a head-on car crash. Marilyn Monroe was found dead of an overdose of barbiturates. Then while running for president, Bobby Kennedy was assassinated, following in his brother's bloody footsteps.

Now it was the sixties, and kids my age were trying to get a handle on all these dreams going up in smoke. Like millions of other teens, I thought I could—we could—change the world. "Never trust anyone over thirty," now a cliché to describe the mind-set of the generation, rang true for me, too.

I remember the first time I saw the Beatles on *The Ed Sullivan Show*. I was living with my grandparents at the time. They were thoroughly disgusted with those four mop-top lads from Liverpool. But I was intrigued by their music and its message—a message that became increasingly drug motivated.

As the Beatles went through their many phases of musical and personal discovery, I followed suit on the heels of a whole generation. We didn't follow the music as much as the musicians—Pied Pipers of a generation playing the sound track to our lives. It was as though an entire generation was caught in an unseen current that pulled us along in an uncertain direction. None of us knew where it was leading, but we were enjoying the ride.

While there are idyllic memories of hot summer days driving to Corona del Mar Beach in southern California, savoring the aroma of Coppertone suntan lotion as I listened to "Surf City" by Jan and Dean on the car radio, there was trouble brewing in paradise.

As did so many others of my generation, I bought into the idea that drugs might contain some of the answers I was looking for, so I could truly "find myself." It seemed that everyone was doing drugs and that drugs were actually being celebrated in our culture. Love beads. Flower power. Long hair. Peace symbols. Psychedelic prints. Bell-bottom jeans.

I followed along at first, almost believing that the answers to the questions would eventually come, as promised. However, it wasn't long before I saw the futility of this lifestyle as I watched my creativity, motivation, and skills diminish. I was told drugs would "make me more aware," and in many ways that was true. I became more aware of how empty and lonely I was deep down inside myself. After a particularly frightening drug-induced experience, I knew that I had to stop doing drugs forever. At that moment I knew drugs would be part of my past, not my present, and certainly not my future.

I had also seen the devastating effects of drugs on the

lives of sixties cult heroes who self-destructed while still in their prime: Janis Joplin, Jimi Hendrix, Jim Morrison . . . all gone.

Add to that the ominous cloud of the Vietnam War that hung over the heads of the nation's young men—including me. We sat in our living rooms watching the daily news reports while the statistics piled up on the latest casualties—guys the same age who had been struggling with the same issues. Every one of us who were draft age lived with the uncertainty that any minute we could be headed for the Orient, right after being hastily taught how to handle a gun.

Then there was Watergate. We watched the highest office in our country unravel and saw a president fall.

All these converging issues caused fear and disillusionment. At a very early age, I found myself asking the Big Questions:

What is the meaning of life?

Why am I here?

And the one that really kept me up nights was, *What will happen after I die?*

The popular belief of our culture seemed to be that once a person died, there was nothing. Life—followed by one big zero. No afterlife. No heaven. No hell. Nothing. A product of the culture, that about sums up what I believed—and the thought of forever nothingness terrified me. How could a person like me—a person with thoughts, dreams, feelings, inspirations—simply cease to *be?*

While I cannot say that I was obsessed by these questions, they did seem to be coming up pretty frequently for a teenager. Interestingly, the person who pointed the way for me to find answers was a girl I'd noticed on my high school campus. It wasn't that she was a beauty queen, although she was attractive. She just seemed to glow from inside herself. And it wasn't that I had a crush on her. I just saw something different about this girl and was determined to find out what it was.

One day my chance came. I saw a friend of mine talking to her and decided to just walk up and casually join the conversation. As I came closer, I noticed she was carrying several books under her arm. One of them was a Bible.

Oh no! I thought. *That means she's one of those . . . those . . . Jesus freaks! That's so sad!*

Nevertheless, I walked boldly over and joined the discussion, just as I had planned, while mentally crossing her off my list of potential girlfriends.

I had seen her kind before—these crazy Christians who would carry their Bibles on campus and constantly talk about God as though he were a next-door neighbor. It all seemed quite insane to me. Don't get me wrong. I believed in the existence of God. In fact, when a crisis hit, he was the first One I called on. But frantic prayers in times of crisis were pretty much the extent of any communications I had with the Almighty.

I had always admired Jesus, too. After all, I had seen all his movies: *The Greatest Story Ever Told, The Robe, King of Kings, Dimetrius and the Gladiators, Ben Hur.* This celluloid Jesus seemed like a decent person. I was always particularly touched by the crucifixion scenes and thought, *What a terrible waste!* I wanted someone to do a contemporary picture, giving the life of Jesus a "new treatment." Why not toss all this death and gore out the window? Why not play up his message of brotherhood and love and just let everyone live happily ever after?

Although I felt certain that Jesus was "out there" somewhere, I certainly did not think he was interested in me or my problems. Anyone who wanted to spend time talking to him—or about him—was fine with me. I just didn't want him pushed off on me. "To each his own" was my motto. I determined to put some distance between me and this young mystery woman—back then we called them "girls."

But several days after having that three-way conversation with her, I spotted her sitting on the front lawn at school—along with about thirty other "Jesus freaks." They were singing songs about God. Already a seasoned people watcher, I determined to study the group from a distance without getting too close. After all, I couldn't sit close enough for any of my friends to think I was one of them. That would have been the equivalent of social suicide in high school.

I watched as passersby would snicker. Even the most abusive remarks seemed to go unnoticed as the group continued their song session. I was touched by their sincerity, even though it struck me as odd that anyone my age would want to spend time singing songs about God. Then a young man stood up with a Bible in his hand. With his shoulder-length hair and beard, he almost looked the way I had seen Jesus depicted in paintings and in the movies. He opened the Bible and began to speak. Although I listened to what he said that day, I don't' remember many of his comments except for one statement: "Jesus said, 'You are either *for* me or *against* me.' What side are *you* on?"

That really struck me. Never before had I heard that faith in Christ was an "either or" deal. Jesus was just this wonderful historical figure who lived a long time ago, did a lot of good turns, and taught brotherly love. As a teenager, I thought that was cool. But for the first time, I had heard that it was actually possible to know him in a personal way. It seemed too good to be true. I looked over at these Christians, all sitting cross-legged in a circle, and thought, *Undoubtedly, they are for him.* Knowing I was not one of them, it dawned on me that this must mean I was *against him.*

This impassioned preacher told the group that anyone who wanted to know Jesus in a personal way should get up and walk forward. Then he would lead in a prayer. I dropped my head and thought, *If it truly is possible to know Jesus in a personal way, I would love that.* Immediately, the doubts came: *What if this isn't real? What if Jesus says no to me? I just can't do it!*

But before I knew quite what was happening, I found myself standing with a handful of other brave souls, praying with the long-haired minister to receive Jesus Christ into my heart and life. I had the distinct sensation that a tremendous weight had been lifted off my shoulders. In no uncertain terms, I knew my life had changed dramatically.

That was in 1970.

But I have never forgotten where I came from or the way I used to think. Because I remember so vividly the path I was on—and the dramatic way my life's course changed—I want to tell my generation that the questions so many people are asking today are the same ones I had once asked.

Eventually each of us asks the Big Questions. Why? Because each of us has the same four basic issues to deal with. Whether we are rich or poor, male or female, famous or unknown, American, European, Asian, African, Latino, white, black, or brown, these four things are true of all humanity:

- Every person, no matter how wealthy or powerful, has an emptiness inside.
- Every person is lonely—lonely in a way that relationships can't fill ... children can't fill ... friends can't fill. I believe it's a loneliness for God.
- There is a sense of guilt in every person.
- Not only are we all empty, lonely, and guilty—everyone of us is also afraid of death.

Many reading this book are probably painfully aware that we no longer have all the time in the world to settle these issues. Some may think they have already blown it. But I have great news: It's not too late to turn it around. Anyone can start over.

Here we are in the twenty-first century (I thought we were all supposed to have personal spaceships by now, just like the Jetsons!), and my generation has finally inherited responsibility for maintaining—and hopefully improving—all those institutions that it once opposed. Now my generation is way past those thirty-year-olds we vowed we would never trust. In fact, some of our children are that age! I heard recently that every eight seconds a baby boomer turns fifty! Now we are the ones in the suits, carrying the briefcases and shuffling off to work. Now we're the ones concerned about house payments and soccer games and carpooling and college tuitions. Now we're the ones wondering how we're going to successfully keep our kids and, yes, grandkids, off drugs, in school, out of trouble, and on the right track. Now we're the ones faced with the challenge of shaping the world for yet another generation to inherit. Indeed, as Bob Dylan used to sing, "The times, they are a-changin'"!

How good will we be at it? Only time will tell. But I know one thing for certain: None of us can do it on our own. We need help—divine intervention. We need to know where we're going, and why. We need a sense of purpose—a goal. We need guidelines.

Where will we find the direction, the purpose, the guidelines we need as we journey into a future racked with rocketing crime rates, AIDS and other mysterious killer viruses, the information explosion, earthquakes, global warming, and Middle East unrest? Personally, I believe we'll find what we are looking for in the pages of the Bible. You might be familiar with its contents—then again, maybe not. This best-selling book of all time contains every problem common to humanity, as well as the solutions. It answers the really Big Questions: *Why am I here? Where am I going? How will I spend eternity?* It contains the answers to lifelong satisfaction, inner peace, and joy. It is as old as time . . . and as fresh as right now. It is for *all time.*

USA Today ran a poll among its readers. They posed the question "What would adults ask God or a supreme being if they could get a direct answer?" Thirty-four percent responded with the question "What's my purpose here?" Nineteen percent would ask, "Will I have life after death?" Six percent would ask, "How long will I live?"

Those are questions that every thinking person gets
around to asking. And the Bible has the answers to those questions. You might say it has first-century solutions to twenty-
first-century problems. Let's explore its contents together as
we tackle the big issues of life.

Any questions?

Greg Laurie
Riverside, California

WHY AM I EMPTY?

It was 2:10 P.M. on a muggy July day in sub-urban Tacoma, Washington, when Mike Kenyon sat down in his orange easy chair and stared down the business end of an L.A.R. Grizzly semiautomatic.

The alcohol, the drugs, the lies, the infidelities were too much for the beleaguered auto mechanic to bear. He wanted to end it all—stop the pain. He pulled halfway back on the four-pound trigger. Then, not really sure why, he put the gun down, turned on the television, and began flipping through the channels. For some reason he stopped channel surfing when he heard my voice and saw me addressing a crowd 1,175 miles away at Anaheim Stadium.

Mike said later that it was as if I were talking just to him that day. He listened as I told the Anaheim crowd that I knew the reality of emptiness, could recall how lonely and painful my own life had been at one time, and could offer a solution to all that hurt, loneliness, guilt, and emptiness. Instead of blowing his brains across the room, Mike Kenyon found the solution he was really searching for that hot July afternoon and took the necessary steps to fill the void in his life.

□ □ □ □ □

How about you? Have you ever been tempted to just cash the whole thing in? Have you ever been torn up inside by a feeling of emptiness? Do you wonder if life has any meaning? Have you ever felt like giving up? There is a solution. It's tried and true. It's guaranteed. It doesn't cost anything, as Mike Kenyon and millions of other fulfilled and happy people around the world have discovered. It's the only cure for one of the world's most commonplace maladies: Emptiness. All of us have experienced it—from the most famous to the completely unknown. We don't all reach the limits that Mike Kenyon reached. Few of us ever get that desperate. But we all know the feeling. It makes no difference whether we're a world leader, Hollywood celebrity, rock star, or a brilliant scientist. That gnawing emptiness can eat away at the soul. It plagues the lifestyles of the "rich and famous" just as surely as the lifestyles of the "poor and unknown."

Emptiness and loneliness are not unique to this generation. Nor were they unique to my generation . . . or the generation before . . . or the generation before that. Nor will they be unique to the next generation and the one following. Every generation has complained of feeling empty because every person is born with an essential emptiness inside—a deep longing for spiritual meaning—an inner vacuum that can only be filled by one thing.

It feels as if there's a hole inside us big enough to drive a truck through. So we follow countless pursuits in our frantic efforts to fill it up. What we want is some sense of purpose and meaning in our lives. We start shoving things into that hole, trying to fill it, stop its aching, close the distance . . . make ourselves happy. What will do the job? Money? Beauty? Fame?

"A Hole in My Life," a song by the Police, might be the anthem of our times.

A one-time leading Hollywood actress told *USA Today:* "It sounds so trendy, California . . . but I believe a lot of us feel a kind of hole in our heart—an unfocused ache that's fixed by some people eating too much, . . . others with freebase. In my case, I'm a romantic junkie."[1]

Actor Nicolas Cage echoed those ideas: "I wonder if there's a hole in the soul of my generation. We've inherited the American dream, but where do we take it? It's not just about cars and wealth. It has to do with freedom. We'll fight for freedom, but are we free in our thoughts, or are we paralyzed by our dreams of consumption?"

Harrison Ford, the most successful actor in the history of Hollywood whose movies have grossed two billion dollars, told a magazine interviewer: "You only want what you ain't got."

What ain't he got? "Peace" was his response.[2]

Media mogul Ted Turner described life as being "like a B-grade movie. You don't want to leave in the middle, but you don't want to see it again." That's a sad commentary on life from one of the world's most successful men.

We sometimes think that if only we had money and fame, we would be happy. If only we could be rich—like Aristotle Onassis—but it was his daughter, Christina, who said, "Happiness is not based on money, and the greatest proof of that is my family." Shortly after making that statement, Christina Onassis died of heart failure reportedly as a result of years of abusing tranquilizers and diet pills.

People have long been trying to fill the emptiness in their lives with things. One of the most popular ways has been with drugs. The list is long of those whose lives ended prematurely due to drug use. So many sixties icons have checked out early. The list just goes on and on: People such as Jerry Garcia—lead guitarist, singer, and founding member of the sixties rock group the Grateful Dead—dead at fifty-three of a heart attack after long years of widely publicized heroin addiction. Garcia was for many a living link to the sixties. Thousands of "Dead Heads" would follow the band's concert circuit across the nation in celebration of the culture and philosophy of that bygone era. Garcia, however, had tried to kick drugs more than once; he had been in and out of drug rehab centers for years.

LSD guru Timothy Leary tried to comfort mourning Dead Heads with a nineties spin on his sixties axiom: "Turn on, tune in, drop out."

"Hang on, hang in, hang out!" Leary advised bereaved Dead Heads.

Jerry Garcia was one in a long line of successful rock and rollers and Hollywood multimillionaires caught in the sixties whose lives ended tragically:

- Rolling Stone Brian Jones, twenty-five—dead from a drug-related drowning
- Keith Moon, thirty-one, drummer for the Who—dead of an overdose

- Sid Vicious, twenty-one, of the Sex Pistols—dead of a heroin overdose
- Elvis Presley, forty-two, the "King of Rock 'N Roll"— dead of heart failure due to drugs

Add to the list rock icons Jimi Hendrix, Janis Joplin, and Jim Morrison, comedian John Belushi, and actor River Phoenix. This list is by no means complete; it is just a sample of the many lives tragically ended due to drugs. And still drug use continues to spread.

> WE SOMETIMES THINK THAT IF ONLY WE HAD MONEY AND FAME, WE WOULD BE HAPPY. IF ONLY WE COULD BE RICH—LIKE ARISTOTLE ONASSIS.

Or take the example of Kurt Cobain, the leader of the platinum-selling rock band Nirvana. He made a career by singing about confusion and frustration. Then one day at the age of twenty-seven, Kurt Cobain took out a shotgun and killed himself in his Seattle home. Ironically, he was only a year younger than Janis Joplin and Jimi Hendrix when they died.

Here was a man who had so much. He had success. He had fame. Yet his life was empty—so empty, in fact, that he had begun killing himself with a heroin addiction long before he finally pulled that shotgun trigger. Cobain reportedly wanted to title one of his albums "I Hate Myself and I Want to Die." In his suicide note he wrote: "I must be one of those narcissists who only appreciate things when they are alone. I'm too sensitive. I haven't felt the excitement for too many years now."[3]

His mother was quoted in a newspaper saying, "Now he is gone and has joined the stupid club." Referring to other rock stars, such as Jim Morrison, Jimi Hendrix, and Janis Joplin, who died young, she said, "I told him not to join the stupid club."[4]

Courtney Love, the widow of Kurt Cobain, said in an interview that appeared in *Rolling Stone* magazine, "I don't think God necessarily put us here to be sober all the time, but I also don't think he put us here to be junkies."[5]

Reflecting on Cobain's death, John Carlson wrote: "In a sense, Cobain is what the spirit of the sixties once envisioned: complete freedom from social, moral, or political constraint, almost universal license to compose and explore whatever landscape he chose, liberation from middle America and its traditional values."[6] No boundaries. No sets of absolutes. And so Cobain's life came to a tragic end. Clearly, there's more to life than economics—than material possessions.

Shortly after Cobain's death, former president Bill Clinton had his infamous encounter with MTV. A young person in that audience raised the issue of Cobain's death. The seventeen-year-old made this statement about her own generation: "It seems to me that Kurt Cobain's recent suicide exemplified the emptiness that many in our generation feel."

Pop icon Madonna was asked the question "Are you a happy person?" She replied, "I'm a tormented person. I have a lot of demons I'm wrestling with. But I want to be happy. I have moments of happiness. I'm working toward knowing myself, and I'm assuming that will bring me happiness."[7]

Apparently fame does not necessarily equate with happiness, as another cultural icon will readily testify. "I feel something's missing," successful actor-comedian Eddie Murphy told *People* magazine. "I don't think there's anyone who feels like there isn't something missing in their life. No matter how much money you make, or how many cars or houses you have, or how many people you make happy, life isn't perfect for anybody."[8]

Another Hollywood celebrity discovered that fame and fortune couldn't fill that empty spot deep inside his soul: "I found that I couldn't shove enough drugs, women, cars, stereos, houses, stardom in there to make me feel good. I guess that's why a lot of people overdose—they get to the point where the hole is so big they die."

One of the most successful entertainers ever is Cher. She is now in her fifties. On growing older Cher said, "I hate my fifties. . . . I never felt older until I hit fifty." She is now building a fourteen-thousand-square-foot, seven-bedroom house overlooking the ocean in Malibu. "When you turn this age, possibilities have become probabilities, certainties," she says. "You've been there, done that: bought the T-shirt, got the poster, been the poster. You have to figure out new, creative ways to stay vital, interested, have new dreams. Maybe next time I'll come back as a cowboy. Maybe next time I'll do better."[9] There's that emptiness again.

Comedian and actor Jim Carrey has certainly had his share of success. His films have grossed millions, and he is one of the higher-paid actors in Hollywood today. A journalist who interviewed Carrey noted, "There's a perception in show business that all comedians are really clowns crying on the inside. And Carrey insists it's true." The journalist wrote: "There is something almost disarming about how up-front Carrey is

7

about past bouts with depression, self-loathing, and even his self-medication through marijuana." Elaborating on some of his bleaker moments, Carrey says, "You have to go through your periods where you cry and sob and scream. I've gone on little personal vacations where I'll go away all by myself and sit and curse at the TV for the whole weekend."[10] I guess even really funny people can be really sad.

Jonathan David, of the rock band KORN, was on MTV holding and kissing a bottle of PROZAC and was quoted as saying, "This is my best friend. I don't know true happiness. I'm not a happy person. I play like it. I act like it a lot. But inside, actually I'm really not that happy."

It's not just the fast lane of Hollywood stardom that leaves this void in people. It touches even world leaders. At the pinnacle of his career as president of the Philippines, Ferdinand Marcos wrote: "I am president. I am the most powerful man in the Philippines. All that I have dreamt of, I have. But I feel a discontent."

That feeling of discontent, restlessness, and disappointment plagued J. Robert Oppenheimer, the director of the Los Alamos, New Mexico, research team for the Manhattan Project, which produced the atom bomb. When asked about his achievements a year before he died in 1966, he replied, "I am a complete failure! They leave on the tongue only the taste of ashes."

All of us have something we live for—some passion, some ideal that drives us. Otherwise, we're not really living, just existing. We all hope when our lives are over that we will have been more than just a statistic—a few lines on the obituary page.

What is your master passion right now? What do you live for? What is it that you think about constantly? What is it that you dream about—long for? What is it that moves you? What is your reason for living?

This is an especially important question for young people to consider. Whatever one's master passion, it is certain to affect the years to come. It will influence the direction one's life will take.

If we were to take stock of the lives of some of those around us, examine their priorities, and look at what they dream about, think about, wish for, it would often come down to a desire to accumulate wealth and property. Few admit it.

> ALL OF US HAVE SOMETHING WE LIVE FOR—SOME PASSION, SOME IDEAL THAT DRIVES US.

But some people do admit it. We've all heard the saying He who dies with the most toys wins. That's the motto of some people today. To them, life is just a big high-stakes game. But the problem with this mind-set is that there is never enough—the drive to accumulate more always overshadows the ability to enjoy what has already been accumulated!

It reminds me of a particularly great Christmas when I was a little boy. I really took in a fantastic haul that year. I was so happy with all of the presents that I had received—until I went to visit my friend. He got something I didn't get. I even remember what it was—a plastic scuba diving figure that would move its fins back and forth when placed in water. For some reason back then it seemed to be the greatest thing I had ever seen in my life. All my other new toys seemed comparatively meaningless after seeing this fabulous object of my desire. Immediately, I started bugging my mom to get me this toy—on top of everything else I had just received.

But we outgrow those bouts of covetousness when we get older—don't we? Not necessarily. No matter how old we get, we still experience that feeling.

You're happy with your car. It's the greatest. It performs so well. And then your friend gets the next new model—or one that's more powerful with a few more upgrades. Suddenly your car just doesn't make you happy anymore.

The same principle applies to other areas of life. We start looking at our friend's husband or wife and think, *Wow, I wish I could trade my husband in on him,* or, *Boy, I wish I was married to her.*

This materialistic and lustful nature isn't a problem only among the affluent. Some people have very little but are actually more materialistic by nature than those who have managed to accumulate many possessions. You can't judge people's hearts by the size of their estates. You may look at someone who drives a luxury automobile and lives in a sprawling estate and decide that that person is very materialistic.

That may or may not be true. Someone with nothing who dreams about material possessions all the time may be more materialistic than the person behind the gate of that magnificent estate. Some people spend all their time dreaming and never manage to accumulate anything. Those who spend excessive amounts on the lottery hoping for the big win are often more materialistic than the guy who works hard for the money to support his family.

One of the wealthiest men who ever lived was King Solomon. In his quest for fulfillment and the meaning of life, he accumulated a vast number of possessions. One day he looked at all he owned—probably everything his eye could see, from beautiful orchards to elaborate edifices. After surveying his great wealth, he said, "Whatever my eyes desired I did not keep from them. I did not withhold my heart from any pleasure. . . . Then I looked on all the works that my hands had done. . . . And indeed all was vanity and grasping for the wind" (Ecclesiastes 2:10-11).

□ □ □ □ □

Some people live for pleasure. This is not a new idea. The pleasure mania we see in the United States today—the hedonism—is not unique to this generation. Caesar Nero, the emperor of Rome, believed the pursuit of pleasure was what life was all about: To live was to be like an unbridled animal in pleasure, passion, and partying. That's the way Nero saw things. That's the way he lived—for pleasure, passion, and parties.

Things haven't really changed much since then. Every generation thinks they have some new outlook on life or a new purpose. But, as Solomon said, history merely repeats itself. Nothing under the sun is truly new; it has all been said or done before: "There is nothing new under the sun" (Ecclesiastes 1:9). Generation after generation, humanity has bought into the same old lies and empty pursuits.

King Solomon, who had known his own share of pleasure mania, said to himself, "'Come now, I will test you with mirth; therefore enjoy pleasure'; but surely, this also was vanity. I said of laughter—'Madness!'; and of mirth, 'What does it accomplish?'" (Ecclesiastes 2:1-2).

Maybe you don't live for pleasure. Maybe you live to acquire knowledge. Now, getting a good education is a wonderful objective—a noble pursuit. A great first-century philosopher by the name of Seneca said, "Life is to enjoy oneself in the realm of ideas. To think. To learn. To master the laws of nature and make the mind the master of man." That sounds good. But is it enough? Can't this pursuit, too, lead to a dead end?

Solomon followed this path as well. Not only was he one of the wealthiest men who ever lived, he was also one of the wisest. He was renowned worldwide for his wisdom. Here is what he said about the realm of ideas: "'Look, I have attained greatness, and have gained more wisdom than all who were before in Jerusalem. My heart has understood great wisdom and knowledge.'. . . I perceived that this also is grasping for the wind" (Ecclesiastes 1:16-17).

Solomon isn't saying that the pursuit of knowledge is wrong—only that if we neglect God in the process, it will be an empty and futile search.

□ □ □ □ □

Maybe you're one of those people who just lives to be happy. Lots of people appear to be doing this today. If you ask them what they are living for, they will say, "Happiness." But, if you ask them what happiness is, they're not able to readily define it.

What is happiness? I don't know—but I'm looking for it.

British novelist William Boyd says, "We all want to be happy, and we're all going to die. . . . You might say these are the only two unchallengeably true facts that apply to every human being on the planet."[11]

Happiness is an elusive thing. I'm not even sure what it is. Is it an emotion? a feeling? a sense of well-being? Maybe it's one of those qualities that people can't define but everyone recognizes readily when they encounter it.

Philosopher Eric Hoffer wrote: "The search for happiness is one of the chief sources of unhappiness."

Maybe you're like Madonna—searching for happiness by trying to get to know yourself better. If so, you may wind up very disappointed. In fact, the more you get to know yourself, the more disappointed you may become. Why? Because the Bible tells us, "The heart is deceitful above all things, and desperately wicked" (Jeremiah 17:9). Every person was born with a sinful nature.

We often hear people saying that they need to "find themselves." But that statement is exactly contrary to what the Bible instructs us to do. Jesus said, "You need to lose yourself."

He said, "If anyone desires to come after Me, let him deny himself, and take up his cross, and follow Me. For whoever desires to save his life will lose it, and whoever loses his life for My sake will find it" (Matthew 16:24-25). In other words, forget about yourself.

We find what we are looking for, not by seeking it, but by seeking God. We don't find life and happiness by seeking those things. We find life and happiness by seeking God, not our inner selves.

Maybe that's one of the reasons so many marriages fall apart today. Too many people enter into marriage unprepared to give, filled with only the expectation of getting. "What's in it for me?" Our modern-day heroes—our icons—provide the worst examples for our culture. It seems that every day we read in the newspapers that another Hollywood marriage is falling apart. Some of them last only weeks or months.

> ACCORDING TO THE SCRIPTURES, TRUE HAPPINESS IS NEVER SOMETHING THAT SHOULD BE SOUGHT DIRECTLY. IT IS ALWAYS THE RESULT OF SEEKING SOMETHING ELSE.

I once heard a story about a distraught and unhappy man who went to see a counselor in search of help and direction. Evaluating the miserable condition of this young man, the counselor said, "Forget about all those things. Go and see the comedian who is performing at the local comedy club. I hear he is keeping everyone in stitches. Go listen to him, and you will forget about all your troubles." There was a moment of silence, and then the client groaned, "I am that comedian!"

Clearly, the world's version of happiness is vastly different than God's version. The happiness of this world is dependent upon things happening. It hinges on things going well. If I am in good health, the bills are paid, and I am feeling fine, then perhaps I am happy today. But if something goes wrong, if someone cuts me off on the freeway, or if I get a cold or something worse, suddenly I am unhappy.

But the Bible gives a completely different view of this elusive thing called happiness. According to the Scriptures, true happiness is never something that should be sought directly. It is always the result of seeking something else. Think about it. When we are trying to be happy—trying to be fulfilled—we rarely are. But when we forget about those things and get back to the purpose for which God placed us on this earth, we find the wonderful by-product of happiness. That's when our lives find their proper balance.

Apart from Jesus Christ, everyone is spiritually destitute. Regardless of education, accomplishments, or religious knowledge, all are empty without God. And most of us have a hard time admitting this fact. It's hard for us to acknowledge our need to reach out to God.

□ □ □ □ □

Dramatic changes took place in the life of Mike Kenyon once he made his peace with God. Some of the changes that followed his decision included the restoration of his marriage and a reconciliation with his father from whom he had been estranged for years. Those who know Mike Kenyon have stated that his transformation has been nothing short of miraculous.

Mike Kenyon says he no longer has an empty hole inside. The hurt is gone, and so are the drugs and alcohol. He reports that he doesn't miss anything about his old lifestyle.

Was it a miracle that saved him that hot July day when he pressed that gun to his head and began to pull the trigger? Yes, it was a miracle. Mike Kenyon was saved by the grace of God.

When he visited California, he handed me the bullet that was in the chamber of the gun he had pressed to his temple that summer day in 1993. I've kept it as a constant reminder of God's power to transform people's lives. This kind of miraculous transformation is available to everyone. It happened to me at the age of seventeen. It can happen to you, too.

WHY AM I LONELY?

CHAPTER 2

One of the last things the King of Rock 'N Roll, Elvis Presley, ever wrote was a note that he crumpled up and threw away. According to a story that appeared in USA Today, an aide saw Elvis discard the note and retrieved it. It read: "I feel so alone sometimes. The night is quiet for me. I'd love to be able to sleep. I am glad that everyone is gone now. I'll probably not rest. I have no need for all this. Help me, Lord."[1]

When he sang, "Are You Lonesome Tonight?" girls would swoon. But apparently Elvis was one of the loneliest people of all. Here was a man practically worshiped by millions. Yet with all of his fame and fortune, power and popularity, he felt alone . . . isolated . . . miserable.

It's not surprising, then, that when a noted psychiatrist was once asked what he believed to be the greatest problem facing his patients, the response was simple and stunning: Loneliness.

7

Others in the psychiatric field will agree that loneliness is the most devastating malady of our age. It has reached epidemic proportions.

Approximately six hundred thousand teens try to take their lives every year—with about six thousand of them succeeding. Why? Loneliness. This suicide rate is unprecedented in human history for this age group. The overwhelming reason teens give is that they feel lonely and isolated and think nobody understands them. They feel forgotten and anonymous. But teens are not the only ones who feel these powerful emotions.

> DO YOU KNOW WHAT IT IS LIKE TO BE LONELY—TO BE HURTING, TO BE REJECTED?

"The whole conviction of my life now rests upon the belief [that loneliness] far from being a rare and curious phenomenon peculiar to myself and a few other solitary men is an essential and inevitable fact of human existence," wrote novelist Tom Wolfe. "We all experience [loneliness] at one time or another."

Loneliness is one of society's chief problems. A study by the American Council of Life Insurance reported that the loneliest group in America are college students. Others high on the list were divorced people, single mothers, housewives, and the elderly. According to the study, the main reason that teens commit suicide is loneliness. Another study found that 90 percent of suicidal adolescents believed their families did not understand them. They said they felt isolated, anonymous, and unable to communicate feelings of unhappiness, frustration, and failure to their parents—who seemed to be striving through their children for the success they themselves had never been able to achieve.

Even the famous and intelligent complain of being lonely. The great physicist Albert Einstein once wrote: "It is strange to be known so universally and yet to be so lonely."

Loneliness wound up being big business for one enterprising individual who placed an ad in the Classified section of a newspaper. The ad read: "I Will Listen to You Talk for Thirty Minutes without Comment for $5."

This person received ten to twenty calls a day in response. Evidently the pain of loneliness was so sharp that these poor souls were willing to try almost anything just for a half hour of companionship.

Everyone knows what it's like to experience loneliness. You can be in a crowded room, and suddenly a momentary loneliness sweeps over you. You just feel so alone. You feel like there's no one—but you.

Loneliness is also a reason why people get emotionally or sexually involved outside of marriage. Often girls are sweet-talked by guys to jump into bed with them. It's been said that men give love to get sex and girls give sex to get love. Think about that. A guy might say to a girl, "I love you so much! You're the girl of my dreams. I'll marry you." But those promises are rarely if ever remembered the next day. Many girls will agree to have sex in hopes of receiving that love. They want to be appreciated. They feel the need to be cared for. They want someone to be concerned about them. It all comes down to loneliness.

Do you know what it is like to be lonely—to be hurting, to

be rejected? Maybe you were not the "big man on campus" when you were in school. Maybe you were not the "prom queen." Maybe you were not the center of attention. Perhaps when you were growing up, your parents moved around—so you changed schools like I did and were moving to new neighborhoods so frequently that you never had a chance to form lasting friendships.

That's what my upbringing was like. It seemed that more people knew me as "the new kid" than by my first name. That's how often I moved. I lived in New Jersey. I lived in Hawaii. I lived in California. I lived in Texas. I know what it's like to walk into a classroom where everyone knows each other—except me.

Of course, that's normal on the first day of school because other new kids are enrolling, too. But when you walk in after the school year is in progress, everyone sizes you up. As you walk to your desk, you can hear the other kids mutter, "New kid." Maybe that describes you—that perennial "new kid on the block," the one who never really makes the connections with friends.

Maybe when they were picking teams for baseball or some other sport, you were always the last one picked. Did you fit into that category? I sure did. They always chose me for first base—not to play first base but to be first base!

Everyone knows what it is like to be lonely—to be the nerd or the geek, to be ridiculed and cast off. But you may be surprised to find that no one knows more about loneliness than Jesus Christ.

"What would Jesus know about loneliness?" you might ask. "He is up there in heaven with all of those angels. How could he ever feel alone?" When he walked on this earth, the Bible tells us that he was "despised and rejected of men . . . and acquainted with grief" (Isaiah 53:3). When he was trudging toward the cross, not only the multitudes turned against him but also his own disciples, who had pledged their undying loyalty abandoned him for a time. Then when he hung on the cross and took all the sin of the world upon himself, he was even abandoned momentarily by God the Father and cried out the words "My God, My God, why have You forsaken Me?" (Mark 15:34). Believe me, there has never been a person more lonely than Jesus as he hung on the cross, bearing the sin of humanity. He knows quite personally what it is like to be alone.

But here's the good news: When you come into a relationship with Jesus Christ and invite him into your life, you will never be alone again. Never. He doesn't promise that you will never have another problem. He doesn't promise you will live on easy street. He tells you that you may well experience hardship in your lifetime. You will have difficulties in life. But he promises, under all circumstances, "I will never leave you nor forsake you" (Hebrews 13:5). Jesus is there. No matter what you are going through, when you have Jesus Christ in your life, you have someone with you constantly—someone who cares.

Those who are not Christians do not have that hope. They are alone—separated from God by sin.

Once we receive Jesus Christ into our lives, we will never be alone again. Of course, that will also include the greatest hope of all—that when we die, we will spend eternity with him in heaven.

That was the great hope that a lonely man named Zacchaeus discovered the day he met Jesus.

□ □ □ □ □

Then Jesus entered and passed through Jericho. Now behold, there was a man named Zacchaeus who was a chief tax collector, and he was rich. And he sought to see who Jesus was, but could not because of the crowd, for he was of short stature. So he ran ahead and climbed up into a sycamore tree to see Him, for He was going to pass that way. And when Jesus came to the place, He looked up and saw him, and said to him, "Zacchaeus, make haste and come down, for today I must stay at your house." So he made haste and came down, and received Him joyfully. But when they saw it, they all complained, saying, "He has gone to be a guest with a man who is a sinner." Then Zacchaeus stood and said to the Lord, "Look, Lord, I give half of my goods to the poor; and if I have taken anything from anyone by false accusation, I restore fourfold." And Jesus said to him, "Today salvation has come to this house, because he also is a son of Abraham; for the Son of Man has come to seek and to save that which was lost." (Luke 19:1-10)

Notice that Zacchaeus was a tax collector. Not only that, but he was the chief tax collector. By definition in ancient Israel this means that he most likely was a very lonely and isolated man. The Roman government had usurped the authority of the Jews in the land. They forced the Jewish people to pay exorbitant taxes to the foreign occupying imperial power of Rome. The Romans hired many to collect taxes—and some of them were Jews. Thus, because of his occupation, Zacchaeus was hated and reviled by his own people because he was a Jew serving the Roman cause.

So Zacchaeus surely would have been perceived by his fellow Jews as a traitor—a turncoat, a person who had abandoned his faith and his roots for mere money. To be chief tax collector could only mean one thing: Zacchaeus had to be skimming off the top. Tax collectors in those days weren't paid a salary. Instead, they could simply add a surcharge of any amount to the Roman tax. If one became rich in this profession, as Zacchaeus did, it meant he was adding quite a markup to the standard taxation rate. As Zacchaeus moved up in his profession, he no doubt stepped on the heads of a number of people. Thus, it appears he had no one with whom to share his wealth. He had no friends and most likely had many enemies. When they spoke his name in Israel, it was with scorn and bitterness.

Now notice when Jesus looked at Zacchaeus, he assessed his lot in life. "The Son of Man has come to seek and to save that which was lost" (Luke 19:10). In this context, the word *lost* does not simply mean "misplaced." It actually means "something that is still possessed but has no value."

Do you have anything in your house that has no value to you but you just can't bear to get rid of? Of course you do. These are the things that you just can't give away or sell at your annual garage sale—broken clocks that are right twice a day, those wire coat hangers that seem inexplicably to reproduce themselves in your closet overnight, socks with no match.

We ought to just throw these things away because they are absolutely worthless. But for some unknown reason we save them. We think that perhaps one day these things might become valuable antiques.

This was the imagery Jesus was creating when he referred to Zacchaeus as "lost." Zacchaeus was a creation of God, made in the image of God, but his life had no value. Why was he lost? Because he was not in relationship with God. His life was going nowhere. He had no real purpose other than to serve the interests of Rome—and, of course, his own selfish interests.

Interestingly, Jesus did not say, "This guy is a thief." He didn't say, "He is a rip-off artist." Jesus said this lonely man was simply "lost." He wasn't concerned about the political propriety of his being a tax collector. He wasn't referring to his unpopularity with the people. Jesus was concerned about the state of Zacchaeus's soul.

Keep in mind that when Zacchaeus heard that Jesus was coming to town, he was excited. The Bible says he ran ahead to get a glimpse of him. That makes me wonder: Had someone taken time to tell Zacchaeus about Jesus? Perhaps Zacchaeus had heard about Jesus from Levi, also known as Matthew, who had become a follower of Jesus. Matthew was also a tax collector and, like Zacchaeus, a Jew. He knew what it was like to be isolated and lonely. But one day Jesus walked by the little table of Matthew the tax collector, and he looked into his eyes and said, "Follow Me." That word *looked* in the original Greek language means Jesus "looked right through him." It seems Matthew wasted no time bolting from that table and following Jesus.

Maybe Zacchaeus had heard about Matthew. *Hey, he's a tax collector like me,* Zacchaeus may have reasoned. *Jesus chose him to be a disciple. Who knows, he might even call me.* In any case Zacchaeus knew Jesus was coming, and he wanted a front-row seat. He found it in a sycamore tree, where he could get a bird's-eye view of this man.

Because of his lonely and rejected state, Zacchaeus may have thought, *No, Jesus would never call me. God could never change my life. Everyone hates me. God probably hates me, too.*

Have you ever felt that way? Have you ever thought that God didn't love you? Perhaps you have thought, *He may love good people or lovable people but not me.*

When I first heard about Jesus Christ I was so cynical. When someone suggested, "Just ask Jesus into your life, and he will forgive you," I thought, *Oh yeah, sure. I'm probably the one guy God would skip!* I was so afraid of rejection that I even believed God would reject me. But I was wrong.

It is likely that Zacchaeus also did not understand God's unconditional love. He climbed up the tree just before Jesus came along. Try to picture what that scene was like. There were hundreds of people pressing around Jesus, wanting to touch him. As they pushed and pulled and grabbed at him, they created a big cloud of dust. And there was Jesus, patiently wading through that teeming sea of humanity.

Zacchaeus gazed down at Jesus from the branches of a tree. Something obviously emanated from him that the tax collector had never seen before in his world of treachery and

greed, something he had seen in no other—a look of unconditional love in Jesus' eyes. Suddenly Jesus stopped, looked up,
and called out his name: "Zacchaeus!" Can you imagine how
this tax collector felt? "Zacchaeus, come down! Hurry up! I am
coming over to your house for a meal."

What's so important about that moment? It represents
the people in our lives whom we think would never be interested in Jesus Christ. If we see someone sitting on the street,
down and out, we think, *That person needs to hear the gospel.*
But if we see another person tooling by in a Rolls Royce, talking on a cellular phone, we might think, *That person would never
listen to the gospel.* After all, how would we ever break the ice with
someone like that? To approach a rich person is much harder—or
so it seems.

It's amazing how many affluent people complain of being
empty and miserable inside. Secretly, they confide they are not
really sure whom they can trust to love and accept them for who
they are, rather than how much they're worth. Tobacco heiress
Doris Duke was a good example. Worth one billion dollars when she died in 1993, the heiress
lived a life of luxury but found that even a billion dollars
couldn't buy happiness, meaning, or peace.

She once told a friend that her vast fortune had actually

> TOBACCO HEIRESS DORIS DUKE— WORTH ONE BILLION DOLLARS WHEN SHE DIED— LIVED A LIFE OF LUXURY BUT FOUND THAT EVEN A BILLION DOLLARS COULDN'T BUY HAPPINESS, MEANING, OR PEACE.

proven to be a barrier to personal fulfillment: "All that money is a problem sometimes. It happens every time. After I've gone out with a man a few times, he starts to tell me how much he loves me. But how can I know if he really means it? How can I ever be sure?"

Most of us struggle with loneliness from time to time. No one is exempt. Here was Zacchaeus—an empty, lonely, guilty, and fearful man. Jesus reached out to him just as he reaches out to each one of us today. In Zacchaeus's case, he was called by name. Jesus said, "I'm inviting myself over to your house for dinner."

Imagine how your spouse would feel if you brought Jesus home for dinner unexpectedly. Wives fear husbands' bringing over some friend without warning—or maybe the boss. But imagine what it would be like coming home and saying, "Honey, I'm home. I brought a guest with me."

"Whom did you bring, dear?"

"Jesus Christ, the creator of the universe."

If I could live at any other time in human history or get to take one trip backward in a time machine, I would love to have lived during the time of Jesus. I would love to have been able to walk with him, talk with him, and certainly to sit down with him for a meal.

But we don't really need a time machine to do that. In a sense, it can happen for us now. Because Jesus said, "Behold, I stand at the door and knock. If anyone hears My voice and opens the door, I will come in" (Revelation 3:20). He means those words. He will come into your heart—into your life. All you need to do is welcome him.

A question I often hear is this: "If I become a Christian,

will I have to give up anything?" The answer, of course, is yes. I wouldn't be truthful if I didn't say that. Yes, you will have to give up some things. There will be changes in your life. But I assure you that what God will give you instead will be so much better—you won't miss those things you give up.

"I also count all things loss for the excellence of the knowledge of Christ Jesus my Lord, for whom I have suffered the loss of all things, and count them as rubbish, that I may gain Christ," wrote the apostle Paul in Philippians 3:8.

> A QUESTION I OFTEN HEAR IS THIS: "IF I BECOME A CHRISTIAN, WILL I HAVE TO GIVE UP ANYTHING?" THE ANSWER, OF COURSE, IS YES.

Undoubtedly, Zacchaeus's life changed the instant he met Jesus. A crowd most likely gathered outside the house after Jesus and Zacchaeus went inside. They probably speculated on what was transpiring between the notorious tax collector and the Lord. Later, Jesus and Zacchaeus may have walked outside together, Jesus smiling as Zacchaeus told the crowd that he would be returning the money he had unjustly taken from them.

Now that's conversion! Immediate change! Instantaneous!

I've heard people say, "I'm in the process of converting to Christianity." I understand what they are saying. It's true that you may become more aware of your need for God and move in that direction. But the moment you ask God to forgive you of your sin and you turn from it, you will be immediately forgiven—on the spot. That's how quickly conversion takes place. It doesn't take months. It doesn't take years. It doesn't take weeks. It doesn't even take hours. It can happen immediately.

So there's no reason to wait. Jesus is never too busy to meet you.

The Gospel of John tells the story of a man in a seemingly hopeless situation. He was abandoned, uncared for, unable to help himself, and desperately alone.

After this there was a feast of the Jews, and Jesus went up to Jerusalem. Now there is in Jerusalem by the Sheep Gate a pool, which is called in Hebrew, Bethesda, having five porches. In these lay a great multitude of sick people, blind, lame, paralyzed, waiting for the moving of the water. For an angel went down at a certain time into the pool and stirred up the water; then whoever stepped in first, after the stirring of the water, was made well of whatever disease he had. Now a certain man was there who had an infirmity thirty-eight years. When Jesus saw him lying there, and knew that he already had been in that condition a long time, He said to him, "Do you want to be made well?" The sick man answered Him, "Sir, I have no man to put me into the pool when the water is stirred up; but while I am coming, another steps down before me." Jesus said to him, "Rise, take up your bed and walk." And immediately the man was made well, took up his bed, and walked. And that day was the Sabbath. (John 5:1-9)

Here was a man, waiting by this little body of water at Bethesda because he had heard about an angel who from time to time touched the water. Who knows if the angel story was even true? We don't know whether it actually happened or whether this was just an ancient rumor. Whatever the case, the scene around the pool was miserable and tragic. Lots of hurting people with all types of illnesses and problems desperately sought a miracle.

They waited . . . and waited . . . and waited for something to happen.

> GOD UNDERSTANDS LONELINESS. HE KNOWS WHAT IT'S LIKE TO BE ABANDONED.

The cry of this man to Jesus two thousand years ago is still heard around the world today. We can still hear its echo: I have no one. I'm all alone. To this lonely, rejected man, Jesus came.

God understands loneliness. He knows what it's like to be abandoned. When we turn to him in prayer in moments of loneliness, we have his full attention.

The story of the lonely man at the pool begins with the verse: "After this there was a feast of the Jews, and Jesus went up to Jerusalem" (John 5:1). In the original language, this passage of text states that Jesus was acting according to a plan and a purpose. He wasn't wandering aimlessly around Israel. There were no accidents. He had appointments to keep, set long ago in the councils of eternity. He was never late. He worked around the clock. He kept an appointment with Nicodemus at night. He kept another with a woman at a local well. In that story we read that Jesus needed to go to Samaria. He went out of his way to go to this place where Jews normally did not venture. Why? He had an appointment to keep with a spiritually thirsty woman. And on that day at the pool of Bethesda, he had an appointment to keep with a poor, lonely, crippled man who had no one to help him. Jesus often sought out lonely people—people unable to help themselves and those with no friends in sight.

Why did Jesus ask this man if he wanted to be made well? Wasn't it obvious, given his position near the pool why this crippled man was even present? I think it was an honest question, meaning, "Are you content with your condition? Are you willing to put yourself in my hands? Are you willing to change?"

Surprisingly, social scientists have found that some people really don't want to change. Some people really don't want to be made well.

Not everyone wants to change. That's why Jesus asked the crippled man lying near the pool at Bethesda if he wanted to be made well. The man at the pool was simply hoping Jesus might help him get into the water. But Jesus did even more than that. He healed him on the spot, and the man got up and walked.

As a result of the dramatic healing of this poor, distraught man, the religious leaders of the day decided to kill Jesus. It's a good illustration of just how blinding religion can be apart from a real relationship with God. I've seen it happen time and time again. When you tell some people about Jesus, they tell you their religious affiliation—and explain why they don't need him. They think that because they have gone through some ritual, they are automatically right with God.

Here was a dramatic miracle performed by Jesus. But still they did not believe.

On another occasion a man named Lazarus was raised from the dead. What was the reaction of the religious community this time? Again, the religious leaders of the day wanted to kill Jesus for his having performed another great miracle.

Jesus reached out and touched this lonely man at the pool. He changed his life. He can do the same for you. Are you lonely? Could you use a friend? Maybe you are a very popular person. You may have a boyfriend or girlfriend. You may be married. You may have a big family. But there is still a void in your life—there is still loneliness . . . a loneliness for God. No one person can meet that deep need in your life. You were created with that void—and only God can fill it.

Are you a lonely person? You don't have to be. No matter how old or young you are, Jesus Christ will stand by you in your life. He will be the best friend you ever had. Better than that, he will be your Lord. He will give you direction. He will give you purpose. He will be your protector. He will be your provider. He will be everything you need in life, and in addition you will find new friends when you become an active part of a church.

Some people think they have to clean up their lives first—or at least make a few changes before they can come to Christ. No, we are instructed to come as we are—with all of our sins. Do you think God doesn't know about them? He knows everything we have done. He knows each of us better than we know ourselves. And he still loves us.

He will forgive us. The only sin God will not forgive is the sin we do not confess.

The question Jesus asked the lonely man at the pool of Bethesda was, "Do you want to be made well?" In other words, he was asking the man if he wished to be made whole. He's asking you the same question: Do you wish to be made whole?

I will not promise you that if you choose to receive Jesus Christ into your life, you will never face difficulties or that you can set up house on easy street. What I will promise you—on the authority of the Bible—is that if you receive him into your life, you will never be lonely again. Jesus has promised to his own children, "Lo, I am with you always, even to the end of the age" (Matthew 28:20). You have his word on it. You can take that to the bank!

WHY AM I
AFRAID?

CHAPTER 3

*Have you ever been gripped by terror? You
know the feeling—a shiver down your spine
. . . the hair standing up on the back of your
neck . . . your stomach sinking . . . your
mouth dry.*

Maybe you were a crime victim—or afraid you might be. In today's crazy society the statistics show that half of us will face
that prospect some time during our lives. Or maybe you were
gripped with fear over the possibility of losing your spouse to
death or desertion. Or maybe you were on a plane that took
one of those unexpected big dips, and you saw your life flash
before your eyes.

Fear. None of us likes to experience circumstances such
as the ones I just described. Yet, ironically, we spend millions
of our hard-earned dollars to be scared out of our wits. We do
it when we climb into radical rides at amusement parks. We
do it when we go to horror movies. We do it when we read Stephen King books. Why do we do it? Maybe it's because we
know that in these controlled environments, everything will

turn out all right in the end. There's something invigorating about being scared when the threat to life and limb is perceived, not real.

Yet we are living in a culture that is becoming increasingly violent. It's dangerous out there in the real world today. There are some justifiable reasons to fear for our own personal safety.

□ □ □ □ □

Associated with the powerful emotion of fear is worry. When you are gripped by fear about your future, your stomach can get tied up in knots just thinking about the possibilities: What if this happens? What if that happens? A great deal of time and tremendous energy are consumed worrying about what may never actually transpire.

Modern medical research has proven that worry breaks down our resistance to disease. It can actually attack the nervous system, the digestive system, and the circulatory system. Excessive worry can shorten our lives. Some people are probably shortening their lives by worrying about when they are going to die.

"You can worry yourself to death," said Charles Mayo of the famed Mayo Clinic. "But you cannot worry yourself to a longer life."

John Curtis, director of the University of Wisconsin Stress Management Institute, said, "I believe that 90 percent of all stress is brought on not by living in the present moment but by worrying about what has already happened, what is going to happen, or what could happen."

Ann Landers says that of the ten thousand letters she gets each month, one problem dominates: People are afraid. They are afraid of losing their health. They are afraid of losing their wealth. They are afraid of losing their loved ones. But as a child of God, you don't have to be afraid.

Worry is a nonproductive pastime. It has been said that worry is the advanced interest paid on troubles that seldom come. It has also been said that worry is like a rocking chair: You are always moving—but you never get anywhere.

> "YOU CAN WORRY YOURSELF TO DEATH," SAID CHARLES MAYO OF THE FAMED MAYO CLINIC. "BUT YOU CANNOT WORRY YOURSELF TO A LONGER LIFE."

Worry is something that can grip us and overpower us. It is interesting that the word *worry* actually comes from an old English word that means "to choke or strangle." Everyone knows how it feels to be choked and strangled with worries.

Maybe we should follow the example of a man I once heard about. He was a bit of a worrywart. One day a friend noticed that he was not gripped with worry, as usual, and inquired, "You're normally so worked up and worried about the future, but today you seem calm and reserved. What happened?"

"I just got tired of worrying—and hired someone to do it for me," he said.

"Really? And what do you pay this person?" the friend asked.

"I pay him $10,000 a month," said the worrywart.

"You pay him $10,000 a month to worry for you? You don't even earn that kind of money yourself. How are you going to pay him?" asked the friend.

"That's for him to worry about!"

□ □ □ □ □

Back when Jesus walked on earth, people were frightened—people were gripped by worry. These people were oppressed by the Romans after centuries of bondage and hardship at the cruel hands of various tyrants. They were heavily taxed, burdened by Roman law that was often in direct conflict with their own Jewish law, and weighed down with the cares of life. The book of Mark in the New Testament tells us what Jesus did one night to alleviate their fears and worries:

> On the same day, when evening had come, He said to them, "Let us cross over to the other side." Now when they had left the multitude, they took Him along in the boat as He was. And the other little boats were also with Him. And a great windstorm arose, and the waves beat into the boat, so that it was already filling. But He was in the stern, asleep on a pillow. And they awoke Him and said to Him, "Teacher, do You not care that we are perishing?" Then He arose and rebuked the wind, and said to the sea, "Peace, be still!" And the wind ceased and there was a great calm. But He said to them, "Why are you so fearful? How is it that you have no faith?" And they feared ex-

ceedingly, and said to one another, "Who can this be, that even the wind and the sea obey Him?" (Mark 4:35-41)

Keep in mind, some of the disciples were experienced fishermen. They had been through many storms on the Sea of Galilee. It must have been a very harsh storm to make them fear so much.

According to the text, waves were breaking over the boat, filling the vessel with water. Those on board were very much afraid. But they didn't have to be. Why? Because Jesus had said something that they had apparently forgotten: "Let's go to the other side."

He didn't say, "Let's go out to the middle of the Sea of Galilee and all drown together, shall we?"

He didn't say it would be smooth sailing. He didn't say it would be a pleasure cruise. There was no doubt about Jesus' destination.

Did Jesus know the storm was coming? I have to think so. You might even say that it was a part of the day's curriculum— all part of teaching the disciples to stand fast on what they claimed to believe.

Our lives are like that too. We usually don't know when one of life's storms will be blowing our way. We don't know when tragedy will strike—when a crisis will hit—but God knows when the hardships are coming. Not only that, he also knows when we are ready for them.

It's not a question of *whether* storms will come. It's a question of *when*. Every person—believer or not—will be faced with adversity at some time. We can worry about these impending adversities all day long, but it won't do any good. The only thing we can do is prepare for the difficult times and rough waters.

At the conclusion of the Sermon on the Mount, Jesus talked about two men who lived in identical homes. The homes appeared to be the same, at least outwardly, but were built on two totally different foundations. One home was built on a solid foundation of rock. The other was built on a faulty foundation of sand. Jesus described a storm that came suddenly and beat upon both houses. The house built upon sand quickly crumbled. But the house built upon rock stood firm. Jesus said in conclusion that the man who built his house on rock is the person who hears the Word of God and applies it to his life. And the man who builds his house on sand is the person who hears the Word of God and does not apply it.

> WE DON'T KNOW WHEN TRAGEDY WILL STRIKE—BUT GOD KNOWS WHEN THE HARDSHIPS ARE COMING. . . . HE ALSO KNOWS WHEN WE ARE READY FOR THEM.

But notice how both men were hit by the storm—further evidence that every person will from time to time experience hardships. The big question is, how will we react to them when they come? Will they destroy us? Or strengthen us? Will they make us bitter? Or better?

□ □ □ □ □

There is good news for Christians. We know that whatever happens in our lives must first be filtered through a protective screen of God's love. God will not let anything happen in our lives that we are not capable of handling. God is in full control. He's completely aware of all of these storms and tribulations.

The word *oops* is not in God's vocabulary. So when a hardship comes, we know that God has allowed it for a purpose; that he has a plan in mind. Hebrews 12:11 says: "No chastening seems to be joyful for the present, but it is painful; nevertheless, afterward it yields the peaceable fruit of righteousness to those who have been trained by it."

Becoming a Christian will not save you from facing hardships. I will never tell you that becoming a believer will protect you against terminal illness. I will never say that becoming a Christian will immunize you against difficulties in your life or that you won't be faced with financial problems. What I will say is that if you become a Christian, God will see you through whatever storms you face.

We will face obstacles. But we will never have to face them alone. He will walk us through the toughest situations. He will strengthen us through the process, making us more like him. Unbelievers don't have this hope. They are like the man who built his home on crumbling sand.

Lives built on people or possessions or religion can all come crashing down quickly. That is why we must build upon a relationship with Jesus Christ—a rock-solid foundation that will stand the stress of storms.

Often we are so gripped by fear that we cease to think logically and forget God's Word to us. That's exactly what happened to the disciples. Jesus' commandments are also his enablings. Nothing can hinder the working of his plans. First of all, he said, "Let's go to the other side." Second, he was on board with them, which means that no matter what they went through, he was there with them.

If you're a believer, the next time you are in a situation like this—faced with gripping fear—remember these two simple points:

- God will be with you and see you through to the other side; and
- No matter what difficulty you are immersed in, you are going to heaven. That puts things in perspective.

Jesus addressed the fears of his troubled disciples on another evening, too. "Let not your heart be troubled; you believe in God, believe also in Me," he said. "In My Father's house are many mansions; if it were not so, I would have told you. I go to prepare a place for you. And if I go and prepare a place for you, I will come again and receive you to Myself; that where I am, there you may be also" (John 2:1-3).

> WHATEVER YOU ARE CURRENTLY EXPERIENCING IS TEMPORARY AT BEST.

If you are a follower, then these truths apply to you right now. Whatever difficulties you encounter in life, look at them in the light of that great truth. One day you are going to be in the presence of God, where you will spend eternity. Whatever you are currently experiencing is temporary at best. God always finishes what he begins. He is the author and the finisher of our faith (see Hebrews 12:2). The Scripture tells us that he who has begun a good work in us will complete it until the day of Jesus Christ (see Philippians 1:6).

You might be wondering if you will even make it as a Christian. You might be wondering if you will one day stumble and fall away from your faith. You might be worrying that you will become a casualty.

Do you want to make it? Do you want to get to the other side? I know God wants you to get there. He is looking for some cooperation on your part, however. If this is what you want for your life, you will make it, and he will complete the work that he has begun in your life. He will help you. You will get to the other side. He will be with you—every step of the way.

□ □ □ □ □

So what are you afraid of? Being hurt? You might try calling 9-1-1. I don't mean punching up the number on the phone but turning to it in your Bible. That is, 9-1-1, as in Psalm 91:1: "Those who live in the shelter of the Most High will find rest in the shadow of the Almighty" (NLT). If we will meet God's condition of doing that, the remainder of this comforting psalm reminds us of God's promises of protection and provision for the believer: "Do not be afraid of the terrors of the night, nor fear the dangers of the day, nor dread the plague that stalks in darkness, nor the disaster that strikes at midday. Though a thousand fall at your side, though ten thousand are dying around you, these evils will not touch you" (vv. 5-7, NLT). In other words, as a Christian you are indestructible until God is ready to take you home to heaven. There is no cause for fear.

What happens after death? Is there a heaven and a hell? We are reminded of the reality of death on a daily basis. The siren of the ambulance reminds us. The funeral procession reminds us. We drive by cemeteries filled with gravestones. We turn on the television and even watch death happen before our eyes.

Death has certainly become a popular subject of movies and books. Unfortunately, many of these stories relating "out-of-body" experiences are in direct contradiction to Scripture. Yet millions of people who have bought the books and seen the movies claim to have found hope and comfort—false hope and false comfort, in my opinion. Could it simply be a figment of someone's over-active imagination?

Remember how popular the movie *Ghost* was a few years ago? I read about one woman whose child had died in a tragic accident. She was quoted as saying that she went to see the film more than eighty times because it gave her so much hope. But *Ghost* was just the product of a Hollywood screenwriter's imagination. Who wants to put their hope in that? Why should we place our faith in some Hollywood screenwriter or person who speaks of his or her supposed close encounter with eternity?

It's amazing how easily people will believe what the supermarket tabloids say. They will believe what they see in the movies. They will put their faith in popular books. But so many will not look with an open mind at the greatest bestseller of all time—the Bible.

It's actually pretty clear what happens after we die. Yet so many reject the truth. Others prefer not to think about it. My staff once conducted some interviews of students on the campus of the University of California at Riverside. We asked the question: "What do you have to do to go to heaven?" One person said, "Uhh . . . I don't know. I guess be a nice person." Another said, "I think that if there is a God—and I think there might be—he is a loving God, and he will accept everyone, no matter what they have done, just so long as they are a good person." Another responded, "Just be a good person, I guess." That answer comes up frequently. Another said, "Go to church." One person said something shocking: "I really never gave it much thought."

This is a major issue. If you haven't given it much thought by now, you might consider starting soon. Would you get on a 747 piloted by a captain who had really not given much thought to where he was going or whether or not he had enough fuel to get you there? I'd say, "Get me out of this plane!"

But we're talking about eternity—a life that continues forever. It doesn't stop. Yet some people don't give it a thought. They have better things to do—more important matters to consider.

We need to think about this. We ought to know what the Bible—the Book of Life—says about death and eternal life.

Over the years numerous threats have been made against my life. I have been in dangerous situations where I wondered whether I was going to make it out alive. I just tried to keep in mind that if my time was up, then my time was up. There was nothing I could do to change that. If it was not my time, then it was not my time. No one can take my life if it is not the will of God.

But let's consider the worst-case scenario—death. What if I die? Of course, the question is not really *if* but *when*. This may come as a shock to you, but we're all going to die—unless, of course, Jesus returns in our lifetime, which is possible. If he comes for us and we're taken to be with the Lord, we won't die. To be honest with you, however, whether it is by rapture or death, it's just a mode of transportation to get me from point A to point B. I'm going to heaven. I don't care if I get there by rapture or by death.[1] Jesus said, "Do not be afraid; I am the First and the Last. I am He who lives, and was dead, and behold, I am alive forevermore. Amen. And I have the keys of Hades and of Death" (Revelation 1:17-18).

Paul was able to stare death right in the face and not be afraid, but say, "I have fought the good fight, I have finished the race, I have kept the faith. Finally, there is laid up for me the crown of righteousness, which the Lord, the righteous Judge, will give to me on that Day, and not to me only but also to all who have loved His appearing" (2 Timothy 4:7-8).

Once during a trip to England, I went to the British Museum. It was fascinating to look at the relics and ruins of civilizations that have long since vanished. I looked at the artifacts and writings of Egypt—once the most powerful nation on the face of the earth. You could also see the ruins of civilizations like Rome and Greece and their incredible statues and magnificent art. What one sees there is all that was left behind by those who have passed into eternity. But as Christians we have hope that we will go into the presence of the Lord.

Jesus was asleep in the boat with the disciples. Imagine sleeping through a storm like that. The disciples should have taken comfort in the fact that he was there with them. We are safer in the middle of a storm with God than anywhere else without him. If God is with us in a storm, we will get through it one way or another.

But fear filled the hearts of the disciples. They were concerned that Jesus was sleeping. They woke him up. Why? Did they want him to get up and worry with them? I don't really think that they expected him to do what he proceeded to do. When he got up and rebuked the elements, the disciples were in shock. I think they simply wanted him to come up on deck to look at the storm and join their pity party.

Have you ever felt God was asleep on the watch of your life—that he wasn't really paying attention? The Scripture tells us, "He who keeps Israel shall neither slumber nor sleep" (Psalm 121:4).

Jesus tells us to let go of our worries and anxieties. In the Sermon on the Mount, Jesus said,

> *Therefore I say to you, do not worry about your life, what you will eat or what you will drink; nor about your body, what you will put on. Is not life more than food and the body more than clothing? Look at the birds of the air, for they neither sow nor reap nor gather into barns; yet your heavenly Father feeds them. Are you not of more value than they? Which of you by worrying can add one cubit to his stature? So why do you worry about clothing? Consider the lilies of the field, how they grow: they neither toil nor spin; and yet I say to you that even Solomon in all his glory was not arrayed like one of these. Now if God so clothes the grass of the field . . . will He not much more clothe you, O you of little faith? (Matthew 6:25-30)*

Jesus is not saying here that we should just sit around and do nothing. He isn't encouraging laziness. He isn't sug-

47

gesting that we stop caring about our livelihood—about providing for our families. But he is saying that we shouldn't sit around and worry all day long.

Worry doesn't produce anything positive. It is a destructive emotion. Don't worry. Don't get worked up and anxious about what might happen. Just live each day that God has given, and enjoy it. That's the only way to go. As I have already pointed out, fearfulness and worrying can shorten one's life and will certainly make it more miserable. Listen to Philippians 4:6-7: "Be anxious for nothing, but in everything by prayer and supplication, with thanksgiving, let

CHANNEL ALL YOUR ENERGY SPENT WORRYING INTO PRAYER.

your requests be made known to God; and the peace of God, which surpasses all understanding, will guard your hearts and minds through Christ Jesus."

Channel all your energy spent worrying into prayer. Say, "Lord, here is my problem. It bothers me. It has not gone away. It looms ever larger in my path. Thus, I am putting it in your hands. I'm not going to worry, Lord. I am going to trust you. I'm even going to thank you in advance that you know what you are doing. And you will work it out for your own glory."

It's not as easy as it sounds, of course. I'll admit that I can be gripped by worry as easily as anyone. But this is the goal. This is what we need to do to counteract the tendency to worry.

God says that if you choose not to worry but to put that difficult situation in his hands—and praise him in advance that he knows what he is doing—the peace of God will guard your hearts and minds (see Philippians 4:7). That's an interesting phrase in the Greek. It could be translated that God's peace will be "mounted as a garrison" around your hearts and minds. God's peace will actually guard your minds. It will guard your hearts so you will not be devastated by worry. Instead of praying with feelings of doubt, you must thank God in advance because of certain promises he has made in his Word—promises that he is faithful to fulfill.

□ □ □ □ □

Remember that God has given us certain words to encourage us as well. For one thing, we know that he stays closely in touch with what we are going through. Psalm 139:3 says of God: "You comprehend my path and my lying down, and are acquainted with all my ways."

The Bible tells me that he cares about me. I am told in 1 Peter 5:7: "Casting all your care upon Him, for He cares for you." The Bible tells me that no detail escapes his attention. Psalm 147:5 says: "Great is our Lord, and mighty in power; His understanding is infinite."

So we know that God cares about us, that he is continually in touch with us, and that no detail escapes his attention.

The real challenge of Christian living is not to eliminate every uncomfortable circumstance from our lives, but rather to trust our all-powerful, loving heavenly Father to run things through the grid of his will.

In Philippians 4:8 Paul tells us not to worry and adds, "Finally, brethren, whatever things are true, whatever things are noble, whatever things are just, whatever things are pure, whatever things are lovely, whatever things are of good report, if there is any virtue and if there is anything praiseworthy—meditate on these things." In other words, we are not to think about fears and worries but about the things that will strengthen us and build us up.

This advice is in stark contrast to much of the misdirected psychology we so often hear today about recalling past hurts and abuses. Unfortunately, pop psychology has even infiltrated Christianity. Many believers are now trying to get in touch with their "inner child." They are delving into subconscious memories and using hypnosis to discover "past lives." In the process they are creating more problems for themselves—in some cases, imagining things that never happened at all. That's not what we're supposed to do, says Scripture.

> THE REAL CHALLENGE OF CHRISTIAN LIVING IS NOT TO ELIMINATE EVERY UNCOMFORTABLE CIRCUMSTANCE FROM OUR LIVES, BUT RATHER TO TRUST OUR ALL-POWERFUL, LOVING HEAVENLY FATHER TO RUN THINGS THROUGH THE GRID OF HIS WILL.

Of course, those who have not accepted Jesus Christ as Savior ought to be concerned. It's a tough world out there. And none of us has any guarantee that we will live to see tomorrow. Those who have not accepted Christ will not go into his presence when they die but instead face certain judgment that will endure for all eternity. What a tragedy that would be!

WHY AM I HERE?

CHAPTER 4

We are living in the "information age."

As we are now beginning the twenty-first century, it's amazing to think that just two brief generations ago our grandparents may have relied on a horse and buggy or a slow-chugging Model-A Ford to get them from place to place. Today we zoom about above the earth in supersonic jets. While our grandparents relied on word of mouth, newspapers, and the U.S. Mail to get their information, today we just turn on a cable news channel and hear the story as it is breaking.

If you want it even faster, you can log on to the Web. No longer tethered by cords, we can instantly communicate anywhere in the world via e-mail, wireless phones, and personal communicators. The pace is frantic.

This communication revolution has propelled the spread of knowledge more quickly and efficiently than ever before. Facts and figures once available only in the world's greatest libraries are now accessible to anyone with a laptop computer and a modem. The result of all this technology has been an unprecedented explosion of knowledge on a worldwide scale.

But with all this information at our fingertips, are we any closer to the truth? Are people any more satisfied with who they are and why they exist?

Do you need to know the gross national product of Papua New Guinea? Easy. Just get on the Internet. The answers to all your questions—even the most arcane—are available in cyberspace. However, what about a more fundamental question such as Why are we here? Where does one turn for the answers to the ultimate issues of life? Is the information age making such answers easier to obtain, or is the avalanche of data beneath which we are buried merely obscuring the more important eternal truths of life?

The fact is, the world is lost—spiritually lost. This condition is not limited to those who live in the United States. This free-floating lack of focus and direction is a global phenomenon. Meaninglessness plagues the entire human race. Those who do not know the meaning of life are guaranteed to feel alienated, to face despair. Those who fail to find an answer to this important question will find themselves without an anchor—unbound by any moral framework, another casualty of moral relativism.

It is moral relativism—the concept that each of us is capable of individually deciding our own moral code, defining for ourselves what is "right" and "wrong"—that leads to the kind of nihilism we are seeing throughout society today. This rejection of behavioral norms has only led to large-scale violence, degradation, and oppression.

So we have learned to live with preteen pregnancies in near epidemic proportions, drive-by shootings, rampant drug use, child pornography, abortion on demand, suicide machines—every person doing what seems right in his or her own eyes. No longer do these horrific occurrences horrify us. Morality has lost its edge.

◻ ◻ ◻ ◻ ◻

People are either just waiting for the future rather than living in the present or—worse yet—have lost all faith in the future and are living only for today. Teenagers have lost their incentive to delay gratification because they no longer believe in the future. This results in a drop in test scores as students ignore the discipline to study and learn. Husbands and wives have been unwilling to keep their marriage vows and have yielded to the temptation to gratify their impulses and throw caution to the wind. So we now have a generation of young people whose lives, at the earliest stages, have been disrupted and disordered by divorce.

Are you waiting around for a miracle? Are you letting circumstances and fate call the shots in your life? I read an interesting article about a psychologist named William Moulton Marston, who surveyed three thousand people with the question "What are you living for?" He was shocked to find that 94 percent of those polled were simply enduring the present while waiting for the future.

They might have been waiting for children to grow up and leave home. They might have been waiting to take the dream trip. Regardless of why they were waiting or what they were waiting for, they were waiting for something to happen—waiting for tomorrow . . . waiting for next year. But one thing is certain: You cannot live in the present if you are waiting for the future. Again, it's a symptom of a spiritual emptiness—confusion about the meaning of life and uncertainty as to why we are here on earth.

"Never before has one generation of American teenagers been less healthy, less cared for, or less prepared for life than their parents at the same age," concluded a study by the American Medical Association and the National Association of State Boards of Education. More than half the students in junior and senior high school drink, and about five hundred thousand say they go out and get drunk every week. That's another symptom of a deep emptiness and meaninglessness in the lives of our young people.

Alexander Solzhenitsyn saw it coming a long time ago: "The West," he said, "has been undergoing an erosion and obscuring of high moral and ethical ideals. The spiritual axis of life has grown dim."

At the same time, however, people are searching for the lost meaning in their lives. The more one turns to materialism, the more one realizes how unfulfilling it is. Some are returning to the church—and to sound biblical teaching—while others are looking for meaning in all the wrong places.

"We've stripped away what our ancestors saw as essential—the importance of religion and family," says Charles Nuckolls, an anthropologist at Emory University. "People feel they want something they've lost, and they don't remember what it is they've lost. But it has left a gaping hole."

Even a major news magazine like *Newsweek* recognized the key questions that are being raised—questions that need to be answered to satisfy people's hungry souls: "That, in essence, is the seeker's quest: to fill the hole with a new source of meaning. Why are we here? What is the purpose of our existence? The answers change in each generation, but the questions are eternal."

Well, not exactly. The answers never really change—not the right ones anyway.

More than ever Americans of all ages are in what you might call a "search mode" spiritually. In *The Next American Spirituality: Finding God in the Twenty-First Century*, George Gallop pointed out that the percentage of Americans who "completely agree" that "prayer is an important part of my daily life" rose from 41 percent in 1987 to 53 percent in 1997. That's a rise of twelve percentage points! The percentage of those who "completely agree" that they never doubt the existence of God rose eleven points in the same ten years. One-third of all adults report having a mystical or religious experience. Baby boomers are leading the search party for meaning.

> "WE'VE STRIPPED AWAY WHAT OUR ANCESTORS SAW AS ESSENTIAL—THE IMPORTANCE OF RELIGION AND FAMILY," SAYS CHARLES NUCKOLLS, AN ANTHROPOLOGIST AT EMORY UNIVERSITY.

Wade Clark Roof, a professor of religion at the University of California, Santa Barbara, says that our generation is facing up to the reality that jogging, liposuction, and all the brown rice in China can't keep us young forever. "As our bodies fall apart, as they weaken and sag, it speaks of mortality."[1] I don't know about you, but I can relate to that statement. Roof further explains that the baby boomers "are at a point in their

lives where they sense the need for spirituality, but they don't
know where to get it."

□ □ □ □ □

Each of us was created with a specific purpose—to know God.
The first man, Adam, knew God intimately. He walked with
him in the cool of the day, beneath the shade of huge trees in
the Garden of Eden. Adam, to put it bluntly, had it made until
he sinned and the perfect fellowship with God that he had
known was broken. Humanity was never to know this sort of
fellowship with God again—until Jesus' death upon the cross
made atonement for our sin. Now it is once again possible for
us to enjoy friendship with God.

Having found this wonderful relationship with God, the
apostle Paul summed up his attitude toward life in
Philippians 3:13-14: "One thing I do, forgetting those things
which are behind and reaching forward to those things which
are ahead, I press toward the goal for the prize of the upward
call of God in Christ Jesus." Here was a man who knew where
he was going. He knew his purpose. He knew what life was
about, and he knew the meaning of eternal life. He knew what
his objectives were. He knew what his priorities were. He
could say with heartfelt conviction about his spiritual life,
"This is more important to me than anything else in life."

Israel's King David was another who shared this single-
ness of mind and purpose. The great king and psalmist wrote:
"One thing I have desired of the Lord, that I will seek: That I
may dwell in the house of the Lord all the days of my life, to behold the beauty of the Lord, and to inquire in His temple"

(Psalm 27:4). King David was a man who knew what life was really about. He knew where he was going.

Jesus valued this quality, as related in the story of Mary and Martha. In the story of Jesus' visit to the home of the two sisters of Lazarus, we see Martha hurrying frantically around the kitchen, making preparations for the meal about to be served to the Master, Jesus. While Martha is busy about the tasks at hand, her sister, Mary, is sitting passively but raptly at Jesus' feet, listening to him, taking in every detail of his teachings. Martha sees her sister's apparent idleness and complains, " 'Lord, do You not care that my sister has left me to serve alone? Therefore tell her to help me.' And Jesus answered and said to her, 'Martha, Martha, you are worried and troubled about many things. But one thing is needed, and Mary has chosen that good part, which will not be taken away from her' " (Luke 10:40-42).

The word *worry* used by Jesus in this passage means, in the original language, "to be pulled in different directions." In other words, it was Mary who clearly understood her purpose and Martha who had missed the point. Jesus was gently admonishing her, as if to say, "Martha, there is a time to do the dishes; there is a time to prepare meals; and there is a time to just sit and listen—and this is one of those times. Mary understands this." Mary, not Martha, had chosen the correct response to Jesus. Mary's priorities were straight. It was Martha who was going around in circles, expending a whole lot of unnecessary energy going nowhere.

That reminds me of a story I once heard about a farmer who took his dog hunting. He stood, shotgun poised, in some ground cover beside a beautiful, sparkling blue lake. When some ducks flew by overhead, he fired his shotgun, and a duck dropped into the middle of the lake. His dog sprinted toward the lake and, to the farmer's surprise, ran right across the surface of the water, retrieved the duck, and dropped it at the farmer's feet. Thinking he was seeing things, the farmer shot another duck and, just as before, his dog pranced across the surface of the lake, retrieved the duck, and brought it back to the farmer. The shocked farmer couldn't wait to show his friends what this wonderful dog could do. The farmer and two of his friends returned to the lake, shot another duck, and sent the wonder dog after the fallen bird. As the three men watched, the dog did exactly as before—walked on water, retrieved the duck, and dropped it at his master's feet.

Looking over to see his friends' reactions to this incredible feat, the farmer was irritated to see absolutely no reaction! "Didn't you see what my dog just did?" the farmer exclaimed. "Have you ever seen anything like that?" One of his friends paused, looked down at the ground, and drawled, "I don't think your dog knows how to swim!"

Talk about missing the point!

□ □ □ □ □

People are searching for meaning and purpose in unprecedented numbers. As we begin a new millennium, this spiritual searching is certain to increase dramatically. This is good news and bad news; as the search intensifies, those with aberrant, counterfeit messages will also multiply. As never before, the airwaves are inundated with attractive-looking opportunities to "know the future," "dial-a-psychic," dabble in the occult—something that is clearly forbidden in Scripture. Yet those unaware of these biblical prohibitions are wandering into error, as lambs to the slaughter, buying into spiritual-sounding platitudes dressed up to look like truths. Another area where counterfeit messages are emerging is the growing popularity of "cafeteria-style religion," where you pick what you like from a number of spiritual menus.

In my book *The Great Compromise* I dealt with this trend and pointed out how we seem to be searching for a God who will help us feel okay about ourselves. We have given God a contemporary makeover. At the expense of reverence for his sovereignty, we have made God over into a comfortable pal, a user-friendly God who makes allowances for our sin and excuses for our backgrounds—a nonjudgmental God who will easily adapt to our chosen lifestyles and give us "brownie points" for doing a good turn now and then.[2]

On the surface it would appear that America is the most religious nation in the world. About 95 percent of Americans say they believe in God, according to a *U.S. News & World Report* survey. About 60 percent say they attend religious services regularly. Only 9 percent of Americans profess no religion at all. More than 80 percent, including 71 percent of college students, believe that the Bible is the inspired Word of God. That's a rather high percentage. Think about that. More than one-third believe that the Bible should be accepted literally word for word. Another 76 percent believe that God is a heavenly Father who can be reached by prayer. Nine out of ten pray. Eight out of ten believe God works miracles. Seven out of ten believe in life after death.

Perhaps the most amazing statistic to me is that seven

out of eight Americans identify themselves with a Christian denomination. That sounds encouraging. Forty-six percent of Americans say they are born-again Christians. It would seem that America is the most religious nation—even the most Christian nation—in the world.

But then we have other statistics that seem to contradict all of this data. It turns out that 38 percent of Americans say there is no one set of values that is right or wrong. This is inconsistent with the number of people who said they believe the Bible is the inspired Word of God. Another 70 percent say it is up to each individual to determine what is right or wrong.

Of those who say they read the Bible regularly but are uncertain about its features, half could not name any of the four Gospels in the New Testament. The other half could name only one. Fewer than half who say they read the Bible regularly knew who gave the Sermon on the Mount. This statistic simply amazes me.

ACCORDING TO A U.S. NEWS & WORLD REPORT SURVEY, ABOUT 95 PERCENT OF AMERICANS SAY THEY BELIEVE IN GOD.

Of the 60 percent of Americans who attended church last Easter, only one-fourth of them knew what the holiday was all about! These individuals who go through all the right motions but have no real relationship with Christ are missing the crux of Christianity.

I once visited a friend who had a beautiful home in the mountains and a dog who constantly chased his tail. Chasing his tail was this dog's number one pastime. It was the funniest thing to watch—but pathetic too. I don't know whether there was something wrong with this dog or if someone spiked his chow, but this crazy dog got so disoriented while chasing his tail one day that he went right over the side of a very steep hill. It didn't kill him; he climbed back up, recovered, and resumed his favorite pastime—chasing his tail until he couldn't stand up.

When I returned for my next visit, the dog was nowhere around. I had so enjoyed watching this unusual dog that I asked my friend, "Where is that dog of yours—the one that chases its tail?" My friend replied, "He caught it. He finally bit it off and died."

Some of us are like that dog—chasing vain and empty pursuits, running around in circles, going nowhere. Once we finally get what we are after, we are often the worse for it because it causes more pain and misery. If, however, our purpose is to know God, we will not be disappointed. Instead of running around in circles, we will find direction and meaning for our lives.

Sadly, many of us are like Martha in the story of Mary and Martha—tied up with a lot of spiritual-sounding activities, yet really going around and around in circles, getting nowhere. Our lives are unraveling. We lack purpose. We have lost our focus. We have lost our direction. We don't have our priorities straight. We don't have the purpose in our lives that motivated King David or the apostle Paul. We can't say, as Paul did, that "to live is Christ, and to die is gain" (Philippians 1:21).

Why, then, are we here?

□ □ □ □ □

Life in the twenty-first century moves at a pretty frantic pace. Sometimes we expect our relationship with God to fit into our busy schedules. But God doesn't work that way. He won't fax his messages to us or call us on the car phone. He doesn't "do lunch." If we are to have a vital, intimate relationship with him, it will be on his schedule, not ours. We must stop running and slow down long enough to hear him—that is, if we expect to hear him.

Some people are quite vocal about America's Christian roots. However, there are some good reasons to doubt the current level of American citizens' commitment to God: the escalating rate of crime, the decline in moral standards, the dramatic increase in abortions, widespread drug and alcohol abuse, to name a few.

So what's going on here? If all those who claim to be staunch Christians are truly experiencing what they say they are experiencing, wouldn't our nation be in much better shape? Wouldn't we, in fact, be in the midst of a spiritual revival? The only conclusion one can draw is that all those who claim to be Christians are not necessarily living out an active faith. Perhaps most important is that these individuals may not understand what it means to be a Christian or comprehend why belief in Jesus Christ is so essential in the search for meaning in their lives. This is why I feel so great a burden to bring the gospel to this generation. Some say that America has already heard the gospel and that it must now be taken to the rest of the world. Though I would certainly agree there is a need to tell people in every nation about Jesus, I do not honestly think most Americans have really heard—or at the very least do not understand—the gospel message. This is why I travel throughout the country with evangelistic outreaches, called Harvest Crusades. I want to bring clarity and understanding of the gospel to Americans in this generation.

When you ask people what it means to be a Christian, you get some interesting responses. One you hear is, "I was born a Christian." Impossible. No one can be born a Christian. You can be raised by Christian parents. You can go to a Christian school. You can attend a Christian church. But there must come a time in your life when you make a decision, a moment in which you ask the Lord to come into your heart and forgive your sins.

Many people masquerade as Christians. Even the Bible warns of this danger: "Examine yourselves as to whether you are in the faith" (2 Corinthians 13:5). Do you pass the test? Or are you just pretending to be a Christian when actually you aren't one at all?

Is everyone who carries a Bible and says they love God a Christian? Not necessarily.

If you were to ask the average person on the street what you have to do to become a Christian, he might say: "You need to believe in miracles." Someone else might say: "You must believe in heaven and hell." What else? "You must believe Jesus is coming again." Perhaps, "You need to go to church. You need to pray. You need to read the Bible, keep the Ten Commandments, and, perhaps, be baptized and have a change in lifestyle."

This may shock you. Did you know it is possible to do all these things and not necessarily be a Christian? I'm not saying that these things aren't good—or important. In fact, I would say that if you are a Christian, you should do all of these things. But just doing them alone is not enough for salvation.

As for determining who is a Christian and who is not, Jesus said, "You will know them by their fruits" (Matthew 7:16)—that is, by what they are bringing forth from their lives.

So let's do a little "fruit inspection." The Bible is very specific about what defines a Christian. There are five tests described in 1 John to determine if a person really knows God.

- Do you confess Jesus Christ as Lord? First John 4:15 says: "Whoever confesses that Jesus is the Son of God, God abides in him, and he in God."

Most would pass this test rather easily. Most would openly acknowledge that Jesus is the Son of God.

- Are you unhappy or miserable when you are sinning? First John 3:9 says: "Whoever has been born of God does not sin, for His seed remains in him; and he cannot sin, because he has been born of God."

This passage is not saying that a Christian will never sin. In fact, 1 John 1:8 also tells us that "if we say that we have no sin, we deceive ourselves, and the truth is not in us."

It is important to note, however, that there is a big difference between the person who sins and is truly sorry for it and does not want to continue in it and the person who flagrantly, willfully, habitually sins. If you are a true believer, you will be unhappy when you have not confessed your sin to God.

- Do you enjoy fellowship with other believers? First John 5:1 says: "Whoever believes that Jesus is the

Christ is born of God, and everyone who loves Him who begot also loves him who is begotten of Him."

Some people would say that they don't need church. They claim that they can worship God just as easily out on the links or communing with nature somewhere. But I believe a person who is not a regular and active member of a local church will be dramatically hindered in terms of spiritual growth.

- Do you obey Christ's commands? First John 5:3 says: "This is the love of God, that we keep His commandments. And His commandments are not burdensome. For whatever is born of God overcomes the world. And this is the victory that has overcome the world—our faith."

There are so many who speak of their great love for God. But do they do those things contained in his Word?

- Do you love and obey God's Word? First John 2:5 says: "Whoever keeps His word, truly the love of God is perfected in him. By this we know that we are in Him."

A lot of people think they are Christians—say they are Christians—but they could not pass one or more of these tests. These people sit in the pews next to us in church each Sunday. They sing the same songs. They pray the same prayers. They put money in the same offering plates. They go through the same motions. None of that means they have a true and vital relationship with Jesus Christ.

Today, however, just as the Bible predicted, we have believers, unbelievers, and pseudobelievers. What does God think about those pseudobelievers? He thinks they're wasting their time. Those who will not live totally for Jesus may just as well go out into the world and live for themselves. Stop pretending. Stop living behind some religious pretense and playing games. Live it up. Do anything they want . . . and wind up in hell.

> JESUS SAYS HALF COMMITMENT IS COMPLETELY REPUGNANT TO HIM.

Here's what Jesus said about such people: "I could wish you were cold or hot. So then, because you are lukewarm, and neither cold nor hot, I will vomit you out of My mouth" (Revelation 3:15-16). That's a fascinating statement. Jesus is saying that he would rather you be ice-cold than lukewarm. You might expect Jesus to say, "I would prefer you to be hot. Lukewarm is not as good, although I'll accept it. But cold is the worst-case scenario." But that's not what he said. He said it is better to be cold than lukewarm. The world thinks half commitment is better than no commitment. But Jesus says half commitment is completely repugnant to him.

When you're cold or have not yet committed your life to Jesus Christ, there is still hope that you will become aware one day and get hot—that is, become a true believer. But when you're lukewarm, you have just enough religion to pacify you. You think, *This is okay. This is acceptable.*

But this is self-deceiving. Let me give an example. Of the many hundreds of thousands of people who have attended our evangelistic crusades, we find that it is often those who are "ice-cold" that come forward to receive Jesus and begin new lives as "red-hot" Christians. I remember hearing about a limousine driver who had taken some people to the crusade in Anaheim in 1994. While waiting for the people outside the stadium, the air turned chilly, and she walked up to one of the tables where we sell various books, music cassettes, and CDs, along with our Harvest Crusade T-shirts, to find something warm to wear. She asked the lady behind the table if there were any shirts without "religious junk" on them. The woman explained that all the shirts had crusade-related designs. Reluctantly, the limo driver, desperate to keep warm, bought a crusade sweatshirt. The woman behind the table encouraged the lady to go inside. When the evening came to a close, the chauffeur returned to the T-shirt stand. With tears streaming down her face, she told the woman who had previously sold her a sweatshirt that she had gone forward to receive Christ at the invitation. She left her name and phone number, saying that she was very interested in learning as much about Jesus as possible.

But the story doesn't end there. The next night this newly converted limo driver wanted to bring someone else to the crusade to hear the same message that had so dramatically changed her life. Inviting many, she was repeatedly turned down. So she decided to just go by herself. As she drove her limo to Anaheim Stadium, she saw someone hitchhiking. She pulled over and told the hitchhiker she would give him a ride in the limo for free—but would he like to go to the crusade first?

He agreed, probably because of the thrill of riding in a limo. They both went into the crusade, and when I gave the invitation, this man went forward to receive Christ.

That's how quickly someone who is ice-cold can turn red-hot.

I'm concerned for the pseudobeliever who thinks he or she knows it all.

All the things I mentioned earlier are of the greatest importance, but they alone will not necessarily make one a Christian. For doing them is a bit like getting the cart before the horse.

God's forgiveness is not contingent on the work I do for him but rather on the work he has done for me through his death on the cross.

□ □ □ □ □

There is a story in the Old Testament about a great Syrian general, Naaman (see 2 Kings 5:1-15). A decorated war hero, a celebrated leader of his day, a man of fame and fortune, Naaman was stricken with an incurable disease—leprosy—a condition that branded him as "untouchable." He was greatly loved by his people for his valor, yet leprosy marked him, and fear of contracting the dread disease made Naaman a social outcast, regardless of the status he had achieved. Leprosy was a state of living death, ravaging the nervous system, bringing gradual loss of feeling to the extremities and creating horrible-looking boils and sores over the body. The disease literally ate away at the skin and huge chunks of flesh fell away. Plagued with this horrible disease, Naaman heard of a prophet in the land of Israel who had performed many miracles. He prepared an entourage and journeyed to Israel to meet the prophet.

He arrived in a gleaming chariot, clouds of dust flying, no doubt expecting the prophet Elisha to come out to greet him and pronounce an immediate blessing upon him, as befitting a man of his stature and fame. Instead, the prophet sent word through his servant that Naaman was to go down to the nearby Jordan River and dip himself seven times.

"The Jordan River!" Naaman scoffed. "Why should I go to that murky, dirty river? I will go back to Syria. We have much better rivers there."

But as he was preparing to leave, one of his servants said, "Master, why are you being so high and mighty? What if the prophet is right? Why not try it? What do you have to lose?"

Naaman did not want to take the prophet's advice because to follow his instructions would have meant peeling off his armor and exposing the true condition of his diseased body. It would have meant humiliation. Of course, God had designed it that way. Before anyone can be forgiven and cleansed of sin, one must humble himself under the mighty hand of God.

So the great and mighty Naaman—decorated war hero, man of valor—walked down to the Jordan River and removed his glistening armor and his wonderful, expensive garments. He stood there, exposed for what he was—a leper desperately in need of cleansing. Obedient to the prophet's instructions, he dipped himself in the Jordan one . . . two . . . three times . . . four . . . five . . . six times . . . nothing. But the seventh time he came to the surface of the water, his skin was clear and clean! To be cured—to live again—this powerful warrior had to first humble himself before God and man.

There is a lesson here for each of us. If we want to receive cleansing from our sins and enter into a personal relationship with Jesus Christ, we must humble ourselves and be willing to admit our need.

WHAT HAPPENS WHEN I DIE?

CHAPTER 5

You've heard the stories. During open-heart surgery, a patient's EKG line goes flat. Attempts are made to resuscitate the patient, but she's out for several minutes before her heart starts pumping again. When the patient regains consciousness, she recounts a detailed story about an out-of-body experience in which she recalls looking down at her own body on the operating table while floating upward into a tunnel of light.

Others who have had similar experiences talk about traveling to luminous crystal cities, meeting silver-blue spirit beings, and learning of calamities in store for the earth. Some even say they met Elvis. I'm amazed at how many people give credence to the words of those who supposedly have left their bodies, then come back again. As mentioned in an earlier chapter, a number of popular books detail alleged out-of-body experiences in which people claim to have seen "a great light."

These near-death stories have become increasingly

commonplace. Not all of them have happy endings, however. Some of these near-death stories describe a much darker encounter.

That's a side of these experiences that most people don't want to talk about. Dr. Maurice Rawlings extensively researched stories of near-death encounters and found that half of the people had a vision of hell rather than a vision of heaven. After they were resuscitated, some didn't want to admit it. They didn't want to talk about it. They couldn't face up to what they had witnessed. I can understand why.

> A NUMBER OF POPULAR BOOKS DETAIL ALLEGED OUT-OF-BODY EXPERIENCES IN WHICH PEOPLE CLAIM TO HAVE SEEN "A GREAT LIGHT."

Of course, there is also the possibility that some or all of these visions are utter deceptions. What does the Bible tell us about Satan? It tells us he is an "angel of light." He is a great actor—a great deceiver. His goal is to get as many of us as possible to ultimately join him in hell.

In that light, wouldn't you expect Satan to give humanity the message that, "Hey, everything's okay after death. You don't have to worry about changing your behavior—your lifestyle. Just keep doing what you're doing. What's Jesus Christ got to do with anything?"

I don't know if all or any of these people have truly had a vision of hell any more than those who claim to have had a vision of heaven. I believe in the existence of heaven and hell, not because of what someone has said about either of these places, but because God tells us in the Scriptures that they exist.

Satan has even convinced many people on earth that life in hell is going to be one big party. Do you know people who think like that? They say, "When I get to hell, I'm really going to party." Keith Richards of the Rolling Stones, who wrote "Sympathy for the Devil"—perhaps rock and roll's most blatant anthem to Satan—apparently thinks like this. "The devil doesn't bother me," he told *Us* magazine, "it's that God that pisses me off—him and his rain. . . . Doesn't he know who we are? We're the Rolling Stones!"[1] I doubt that will impress God very much. The Stones used to sing a song called "Time Is on My Side." From the apparent way age has diminished their appearance in their latest video, I doubt any of the famous band members could claim that any longer.

But what's with all these near-death experiences? Do they tell us anything about the afterlife? Are they really spiritual experiences? Are they delusions?

Everybody's fascinated with these present-day afterlife experiences. People seem more concerned than ever with the whole idea of death. Just look at the books on the subject and how they are selling. The baby boomers are aging, and death and disease no longer seem to be such remote possibilities. But this is not just a popular question today. It is as old as time itself.

□ □ □ □ □

Hundreds of years ago Job asked a question (in the oldest book of the Bible) that is still being asked today. In spite of all our technology and advances the essential problems and needs of humanity remain the same.

Job's question: "If a man dies, shall he live again?" (Job 14:14).

Rock star Sting recently weighed in with his view of death in a magazine article: "Without wishing to seem morbid, I'm trying to work out how to die well. I'm halfway through my life. Death's a taboo in our society, but let's think about it and work out a strategy. If you want to live well, you must surely want to die well."

Sting is right. Death is clearly unavoidable.

Actor Tobey Maguire, who starred in such films as *Cider-House Rules,* grew up poor and was overwhelmed by his sudden stardom. In the March 2000 issue of *Harper's Bazaar* Maguire, twenty-five, talked about the changes in his life and his role as a suidical writing student in *Wonder Boys:* "Sometimes I get panicky," Maguire said. "I ask myself what life is, you know? Is it the pursuit of material success? Is is a spiritual journey? I'm really learning about responsibility and mortality—these are two big things. The concept that this is not a dress rehearsal." Mortality is something we all should be thinking about.

After the death of Cher's former husband, Sonny Bono, Cher was quoted in an interview as saying, "I know it sounds weird, but how hard can dying be? I figure it's all right because he's done it, and if he can do it, I can do it. I just feel a little less anxious, a bit more comforted about being dead." Recently Cher contacted best-selling psychic James Van Praagh (*Talking to Heaven: A Medium's Message of Life after Death*), who assured her that Sonny told him from beyond "how much he loved her."[2]

Sadly, this is simply not the case. Once we are gone, we are gone. And we or they cannot communicate with people from the other side.

It is so shocking when someone that we may think is beyond the grasp of death is suddenly taken from us. How many of us were shocked when Princess Diana was tragically killed in an automobile accident in Paris, France? Or when JFK Jr., his wife, Caroline, and her sister Lauren were unexpectedly killed when their plane crashed on the way to a wedding? Things like these are not supposed to happen to people so young, vibrant, and famous. After all, Diana was a princess. John Kennedy Jr. was like a prince. Princes and princesses are not supposed to die. At least they don't in fairy tales.

But they live in the same world we live in. And everybody eventually dies. Even princes and princesses. And so will you.

Movies, television, and the popular culture can make death seem so unreal. After all, we still hear the music of John Lennon, Buddy Holly, Jim Morrison, Nat King Cole, and Elvis Presley. We still see John F. Kennedy and Martin Luther King making speeches on TV. We still see James Dean, Marilyn Monroe, and John Wayne in movies.

Before he died, John Wayne told ABC television's Barbara Walters why he didn't like watching his old movies: "It's kind of irritating to me. I was a good-looking forty-year-old, and suddenly I can look over and see this seventy-one-year-old. . . . I'm not squawking. . . . I just want to be around for a long time."

But death knocks at every door. It is no respecter of how famous or wealthy, beautiful, or powerful we were. The Bible teaches there are actually two deaths: One is physical death, and the other is eternal, spiritual death. Jesus warned that we are to fear the second death more than the first death. He discussed the second death as spending eternity in hell, which is eternal separation from God. He indicated that the death of our bodies is nothing compared to the conscious, everlasting banishment of our souls from God.

Many people bristle at the mention of the word *hell*. Hell is a controversial, unpopular subject. But according to the Bible, hell is real. Many think it is nothing more than a joke, imagining it as an eternal party place where the bar never closes.

Woody Allen once said, "Hell is the future abode of all people who personally annoy me." But hell is no joke! In fact, Jesus spoke more about hell than all the other preachers in the Bible put together!

Why? Because he alone has seen it. He knows its horrors, and the last thing he wants is for any person to spend eternity there! God wants us to spend eternity in heaven with him! Jesus prayed, "I desire that they . . . may be with Me . . . and that they may behold My glory" (John 17:24). But if we follow Jesus, death should no longer terrify us. As soon as we are dead we will be with the Lord. Jesus told the repentant thief on the cross, "Today you will be with Me in Paradise" (Luke 23:43).

Paul said that he had "a desire to depart and be with Christ" (Philippians 1:23). He also affirmed, "We are always confident, knowing that while we are at home in the body we are absent from the Lord. For we walk by faith, not by sight. We are confident, yes, well pleased rather to be absent from the body and to be present with the Lord" (2 Corinthians 5:6-8).

In heaven there will be no night. Revelation 22:5 says:

"There shall be no night there: They need no lamp nor light of the sun, for the Lord God gives them light."

There will be no more suffering or death, according to Revelation 21:3-5: "'Behold, the tabernacle of God is with men, and He will dwell with them, and they shall be His people. God Himself will be with them and be their God. And God will wipe away every tear from their eyes; there shall be no more death, nor sorrow, nor crying. There shall be no more pain, for the former things have passed away.' Then He who sat on the throne said, 'Behold, I make all things new.' And He said to me, 'Write, for these words are true and faithful.'"

All our questions will be answered. "For now we see in a mirror, dimly, but then face to face. Now I know in part, but then I shall know just as I also am known" (1 Corinthians 13:12).

But needless to say, the highlight of heaven will be Jesus! The great evangelist D. L. Moody said, "It's not the jeweled walls and pearly gates that are going to make heaven attractive. It is being with God."

□ □ □ □ □

How will you react when death knocks at your door?

Thomas Paine, the renowned American author, exerted considerable influence against God and the Scriptures. He wrote a book called *The Age of Reason*, designed to undermine Christianity. On his deathbed he said, "I would give worlds, if I had them, that *The Age of Reason* had not been published. Oh, Lord, help me! Christ, help me! Oh, God, what have I done to suffer so much? But there is no God! If there should be, what will become of me hereafter? Stay with me, for God's sake. Send even a child to stay with me for it is hell to be alone. If ever the devil had an agent, I have been that one."

Here is a tortured confused man on his deathbed calling out to God, then realizing that he doesn't even believe in God!

Voltaire, the renowned French agnostic, was one of the most aggressive antagonists of Christianity. Like Paine, he wrote things to undermine the church. He once said, "Curse the wretch," speaking of Jesus. "In twenty years, Christianity will be no more. My single hand will destroy the edifice it took twelve apostles to rear." It is truly ironic that the house where Voltaire wrote so many of his anti-God works is still standing and today is home to a small printing endeavor—that produces Bibles!

A nurse who attended Voltaire on his deathbed was reported to have said, "For all the wealth in Europe, I would not see another nonbeliever die."

The physician waiting up with Voltaire at his death said that he cried out most desperately, "I am abandoned by God and man! I will give you half of what I am worth if you will give me six months of life. Then I shall go to hell, and you will go with me. Oh, Christ! Oh, Jesus Christ." No tunnels leading to a great light—just harsh reality.

As he was being stoned to death, Stephen, a martyr during the time of the early apostles, said, "Look! I see the heavens opened and the Son of Man standing at the right hand of God!" (Acts 7:56).

Christians will meet death as did D. L. Moody, whose words on his deathbed were: "I see earth receding, and heaven is opening. God is calling me."

Another Christian who died valiantly during the persecution of Rome was Polycarp, one of my favorite heroes of the church. As an aged man, he was arrested and brought before the Roman counsel in the amphitheater. He was told, "Have respect for your old age! Swear by the genius of Caesar." Polycarp said, "Eighty-six years have I served [Christ], and he has done me no wrong. How can I deny my King who saved me?"

Polycarp was taken to the stake to be burned. The guard who was ordered to torture him said, "I don't want to burn you, old man. The fire will be hot." Polycarp replied, "Not as hot as the fire that those who reject my Lord Jesus Christ will experience!"

> VOLTAIRE CRIED OUT, "I AM ABANDONED BY GOD AND MAN!"

They lit the fire and it encircled him, but the flames did not touch him as he sang songs to God. They thrust him through with a spear, and the blood pouring from his body extinguished the flames. Yes, Polycarp died, but he went to heaven.

Each of us will die sooner or later. We need to accept that without fear. We don't know when death will come. We certainly don't know if we'll have time to wait on making a decision to follow Christ until the end of our lives. None of us can be certain when the end will be.

I once read a fascinating article in *Life* magazine about the aftermath of the crash of flight 232—an aircraft that had an onboard crisis when its hydraulics shut down en route from Denver to Chicago. The people aboard endured forty-one hair-raising minutes before they could land and were aware the entire time that they faced almost certain death. Of the 296 passengers, 180 survived. Here's how some of the survivors reflected upon their near-death experiences.

- One man said the plane smelled like a house after a fire. He added that he could "see and smell" death. He reached for his flight bag and took out a Bible. "That's all I wanted," he said.

- Another passenger said he wrote a letter to his family in the final moments before the crash. As the plane jerked and shuddered erratically, he recalled a cross he carried in his pocket, pulled it out, and held it in his hand for the rest of the trip. "Though I came out with only cuts and bruises, they put me in the hospital for an irregular heartbeat. I thought maybe it would be nice to read the Bible. I hadn't read it in years. I turned to Psalm 121, and it came back to me that I had memorized that psalm."

- A thirty-nine-year-old Detroit woman said, "When the plane crashed, I saw nothing but grass. *Oh God,* I thought, *the peacefulness you have given me!* I said to myself, *Thank you, Jesus,* because I knew there was no other way we would make it."

- One of the flight attendants recalled that she thought about her family and friends as the plane was going down. She thought about the things she hadn't accomplished. She pictured her pastor announcing her death in church but felt at peace. "I thought, *It's okay. The Lord's going to take me and I'll be okay.*"

The disaster produced another touching story. After the crash a little girl whose father had just died asked her mother where her father had gone. "To be with Jesus," replied the mother.

A few days later, talking to a friend, the mother said, "I am so grieved to have lost my husband."

The little girl heard her and, remembering what she had told her, asked, "Mother, is a thing lost when you know where it is?"

"No, of course not," said her mom.

"Well, then, how can Daddy be lost when he has gone to be with Jesus?"

That's the reality. Popular culture fights death at every turn. "Why do we have to die?" asks Mel Brooks. "As a kid you get nice little white shoes with white laces and a velvet suit with short pants and a nice collar. You go to college, meet a nice girl, get married, work a few years, and then you have to die! What is that? . . ."

☐ ☐ ☐ ☐ ☐

There are better places to turn for insight into the afterlife than the stories of near-death experiences or the rantings of heroes of the popular culture. In fact, there are two rather explicit and quite dramatic afterlife experiences described in the Bible:

> There was a certain rich man who was clothed in
> purple and fine linen and fared sumptuously every
> day. But there was a certain beggar named Lazarus,
> full of sores, who was laid at his gate, desiring to be
> fed with the crumbs which fell from the rich man's

table. Moreover the dogs came and licked his sores. So it was that the beggar died, and was carried by the angels to Abraham's bosom. The rich man also died and was buried. And being in torment in Hades, he lifted up his eyes and saw Abraham afar off, and Lazarus in his bosom. Then he cried and said, "Father Abraham, have mercy on me, and send Lazarus that he may dip the tip of his finger in water and cool my tongue; for I am tormented in the flame." But Abraham said, "Son, remember that in your lifetime you received your good things, and likewise Lazarus evil things; but now he is comforted and you are tormented. And besides all this, between us and you there is a great gulf fixed, so that those who want to pass from here to you cannot, nor can those from there pass to us." Then he said, "I beg you therefore, father, that you would send him to my father's house, for I have five brothers, that he may testify to them, lest they also come to this place of torment." Abraham said to him, "They have Moses and the prophets; let them hear them." And he said, "No, father Abraham; but if one goes to them from the dead, they will repent." But he said to him, "If they do not hear Moses and the prophets, neither will they be persuaded though one rise from the dead" (Luke 16:19-31).

Jesus often used parables to illustrate points he wanted to make. They were earthly stories with heavenly meanings—illustrations. This, however, was not a parable. There could be no more authoritative account of life beyond the grave than the eyewitness account given by Jesus himself. In contrast to his parables where people were not named, in this story the characters were clearly named. Therefore, we know this is a real story describing a real situation.

It's the story of two men—one owned everything, yet possessed nothing; the other owned nothing, yet inherited everything. Jesus told this story in the context of an address to people who were obsessed with greed and materialism. He was talking about people being possessed by their possessions.

Jesus did not condemn riches. Being wealthy is not a sin; nor is it a virtue. This is simply a story about a man whose passion was his possessions, rather than God. He was too busy accumulating things to make time for God. The text says he "fared sumptuously." That means he lived flamboyantly. He probably had magnificent banquets every day. All this rich man cared about was finding pleasure in life. He was like a first-century party animal. He was clothed in purple and fine linen, the clothing of royalty. He not only had wealth but he flaunted it.

Meanwhile, outside his gate was an impoverished man named Lazarus. He actually ate the crumbs that fell from the rich man's table. It's interesting because in this ancient culture an affluent person didn't use napkins; he wiped his hands on pieces of bread. The bread was used to absorb the oils on the hands. When he finished, he would throw the bread on the ground. It normally was eaten by dogs. Yet sadly, this was Lazarus's primary diet. He lived on the bread that was used to wipe the food off the wealthy man's hands.

I doubt there was much of a funeral on the day the poor man Lazarus died. After all, he was just a beggar. But death is the great leveler. Beggars die. Rich people die. Rock stars die. Unknown people die. Presidents die. Kings and queens die. Everyone eventually faces death.

Death is no respecter of persons. Money, success, and social standing make no difference when death comes knocking.

> DEATH IS THE GREAT LEVELER. BEGGARS DIE. RICH PEOPLE DIE. ROCK STARS DIE. UNKNOWN PEOPLE DIE. EVERYONE EVENTUALLY FACES DEATH.

Malcolm Forbes. Presidents Kennedy, Johnson, and Nixon. Howard Hughes. John Lennon. Jimi Hendrix. Kurt Cobain. Marilyn Monroe. River Phoenix, Chris Farley, John Belushi, Phil Hartman, Princess Diana, John Kennedy Jr. The list just goes on.

"The rich and the poor have this in common, The Lord is the maker of them all," says Proverbs 22:2.

So the rich man in this story also died, setting up the contrast for Jesus' great parable about heaven and hell. Surely the rich man must have had a grand funeral. He would have been laid in a massive tomb. His relatives no doubt hired professional wailers to mourn for him. That was something the wealthy did in that culture. To make their death processions more memorable, they would pay people to mourn and grieve and cry out loud. But once this man was dead, he had to face the penalty of his sins—alone.

The Bible tells us that the poor man Lazarus was carried by angels to Abraham. One of the purposes of angels is to usher Christians—God's children—into his presence when they die.

But the rich man went to the place of judgment—a place called Hades, where he found himself in torment. This story illustrates that hell is not simply a place devoid of God's presence. It is actually a place of torment and suffering. This story also makes it clear that once in hell, there's no way out. Once in heaven, there's no way to cross over the threshold into hell. So our eternal fate is decided right here on earth in this life—not in some future world.

☐ ☐ ☐ ☐ ☐

It's clear there are only two options—heaven and hell. That's it. There's no middle ground.

Let me explain something about this place called Hades. Both these men were actually in Hades. Before Jesus' death and resurrection, everyone—believers and unbelievers—went to Hades, where there were two sections—one of comfort and the other of torment. Abraham's bosom represented the comfort zone. When Jesus died on the cross, the Scripture tells us he descended into Hades and took those people in Abraham's bosom up to heaven with him. Ever since then, when believers die, they go directly to heaven. When unbelievers die, they still go to Hades. But there's no more comfort zone—it's been permanently closed. There's only the torment zone left—hell.

The word *torment* is used four times in the text of this story. People in hell are fully conscious and in pain. Sinners don't go into suspended animation. They aren't reincarnated.

The rich man in this story was desperate for a drop of water from Lazarus's finger. He wanted someone to warn his brothers, who were still alive, about the terrible fate in store for them if they didn't become reconciled to God. He would like to have gone back himself to warn them. He thought they would listen to someone who rose from the dead.

Interestingly, a different man named Lazarus did rise from the dead. Let's see what happened in John 11:1-15:

Now a certain man was sick, Lazarus of Bethany, the town of Mary and her sister Martha. It was that Mary who anointed the Lord with fragrant oil and wiped His feet with her hair, whose brother Lazarus was sick. Therefore, the sisters sent to Him, saying, "Lord, behold, he whom You love is sick." When Jesus heard that, He said, "This sickness is not unto death, but for the glory of God, that the Son of God may be glorified through it." Now Jesus loved Martha and her sister and Lazarus. So, when He heard that he was sick, He stayed two more days in the place where He was. Then after this He said to the disciples, "Let us go to Judea again." The disciples said to Him, "Rabbi, lately the Jews sought to stone You, and are You going there again?" Jesus answered, "Are there not twelve hours in the day? If anyone walks in the day, he does not stumble, because he sees the light of this world. But if one walks in the night, he stumbles, because the light is not in him." These things He said, and after that He said to them, "Our friend Lazarus sleeps, but I go that I may wake him up." Then His disciples said, "Lord, if he sleeps he will get well." However, Jesus spoke of his death, but they thought that He was speaking about taking rest in sleep. Then Jesus said to them plainly, "Lazarus is dead. And I am glad for your sakes that I was not there, that you may believe. Nevertheless let us go to him."

The text shows that Mary and Martha had called for Jesus and expected him to come immediately and heal Lazarus. But as we've all heard so often, God often works in mysterious ways. The Bible says, "For as the heavens are higher than the earth, so are My ways higher than your ways, and My thoughts than your thoughts" (Isaiah 55:9). There are times in life God doesn't do what we want or expect him to do. We may be disappointed by that. We feel he's let us down.

In this case it's clear that Jesus deliberately delayed his arrival in Bethany until after Lazarus had died. He did this precisely because he loved Lazarus, Mary, and Martha so much.

But when Jesus finally arrived, Martha confronted him: "Lord, if You had been here, my brother would not have died." Martha was clearly a believer. She understood the Lord's miraculous healing power. But she was disappointed. Then she added: "I know that whatever You ask of God, God will give You" (John 11:21-22).

Jesus ordered the stone to be removed from the tomb. But Martha was concerned because Lazarus had been dead for four days. In those days there was no embalming. Decomposition took place rapidly once a corpse was sealed in the tomb.

Nevertheless, Jesus went to the tomb and cried out: "Lazarus, come forth!" (John 11:43). And Lazarus came forth.

Did the people who witnessed this miracle drop to their knees and become believers on the spot? No. In fact, the religious leaders plotted to kill the resurrected Lazarus. He represented a living miracle, and as such was an embarrassment to them (see John 12:10).

> THERE ARE TIMES IN LIFE GOD DOESN'T DO WHAT WE WANT OR EXPECT HIM TO DO. WE MAY BE DISAPPOINTED BY THAT. WE FEEL HE'S LET US DOWN.

Of course, someone greater than Lazarus also rose from the dead. And when Jesus himself came back from the dead, some skeptics still refused to believe.

❑ ❑ ❑ ❑ ❑

Sometimes we think that if only we could perform miracles for our unbelieving friends, we could convince them all—convert them all. If only we could make the blind see or heal a disabled person, surely then every witness would become a believer. Right? Well, maybe not.

Perhaps you have thought, *If only I could have all my friends over for a cookout, throw some burgers on the grill, and ask the Lord to send down fire from heaven, just as he did for the prophet Elijah, then they would believe. After that, for an encore, I could walk across the water of my swimming pool! Surely that would do it! Right?* Wrong. Jesus said, "An evil and adulterous generation seeks after a sign, and no sign will be given to it except the sign of the prophet Jonah. For as Jonah was three days and three nights in the belly of the great fish, so will the Son of Man be three days and three nights in the heart of the earth" (Matthew 12:39-40).

In other words, Jesus said: "You want a miracle? You want a sign? Here it is. I am going to go die on the cross. I am going to pay for the sins of the world. I am going to rise again from the dead." That's it. People will either become believers from hearing that message or they will not. If not, they will wind up in the place of torment—forever.

Right now you may be thinking, *How could a God of love do this? It's not fair. Why should a place like hell exist?* To understand the answers to these questions, one must comprehend the love of God versus the wickedness of sin. God's love is a powerful love—not a shallow sentiment. He is a holy God; therefore, his love for us is holy—completely pure and without sin.

Scripture tells us that "God is light and in Him is no darkness at all" (1 John 1:5). Sin is rebellion against God. Each of us has sinned and fallen short of God's glory. He gives us an opportunity to be forgiven of our sins through his Son. In other words, God doesn't send people to hell. People send themselves to hell by failing to heed God's call and believe in Jesus.

It is not sinful to doubt. In fact, doubt is not necessarily a bad thing. Each of us is faced with skepticism during our lives. But there is a difference between doubt and unbelief. Skepticism and doubt are issues that can be resolved, once the facts are presented. For instance, I have always been a skeptic by nature. I do not believe something immediately, just because someone says it is so. The Bible tells the story of a man named Thomas, often referred to as "doubting Thomas." But he was not a doubter as much as he was a skeptic. He was told by the other disciples that Jesus had risen from the dead and had personally appeared to them. Thomas said, "Unless I see in His hands the prints of the nails, and put my finger into the print of the nails, and put my hand into His side, I will not believe" (John 20:25). Thomas was asking for nothing more than the others had seen. Jesus appeared to the disciples and Thomas eight days later, and when this skeptical man came into contact with the risen Christ, his skepticism gave way to belief.

In contrast, an unbeliever is someone who makes a willful, deliberate choice not to believe. C. S. Lewis said, "The safest road to hell is a gradual one—the gentle slope, soft underfoot, without sudden turnings, without milestones, without signposts. It's that slippery slope that you gradually go down as your life passes by."

We are all headed for one of two destinations in eternity, and it's up to us to determine where we go. The last thing God wants is to see us spend eternity in hell. That is why he took the drastic measure of sending his Son, Jesus, to die on the cross in our place. Jesus Christ, the Son of God, offers you and me pardon and forgiveness. If we will turn from our sin and turn to him by faith, he will forgive us. But if we reject his pardon, turn away from his loving and gracious offer of forgiveness, and choose to spend eternity in hell, we will have no one to blame but ourselves.

The Bible is very clear: There will be a final judgment. Revelation 20:15 gives us a glimpse of it:

I saw a great white throne and Him who sat on it,
from whose face the earth and the heaven fled away.

And there was found no place for them. And I saw the dead, small and great, standing before God, and books were opened. And another book was opened, which is the Book of Life. And the dead were judged according to their works, by the things which were written in the books. The sea gave up the dead who were in it, and Death and Hades delivered up the dead who were in them. And they were judged, each one according to his works. Then Death and Hades were cast into the lake of fire. This is the second death. And anyone not found written in the Book of Life was cast into the lake of fire.

Only unbelievers will be present at this judgment. If unbelievers are already condemned for rejecting Christ, why must they stand before God in judgment? Perhaps to demonstrate to each individual why he or she is condemned. No doubt there will still be those on Judgment Day who will say, "Wait a second here. Stop the presses! What's going on here? I thought all I had to do was be a good person."

The books will be opened. Notice that it refers to "books"—plural. Another book—singular—was opened. This is the Book of Life. There is more than one book. There is the Book of Life. And then there are these other books. But the Bible doesn't tell us what is written in these books. So we can only speculate based on Scripture.

Perhaps one book contains a record of everything we have said or done. Ecclesiastes 12:14 says that God will judge us for everything we do, including every secret thing, good or bad. The Bible also tells us that we will have to give an account of every idle word that we speak. So it is apparent that God keeps records.

Today we have sophisticated computer equipment. We can store incredible amounts of data and keep it all on file. But God has a far more sophisticated record-keeping system, to say the least. According to Scripture, everything we do, every word we speak, is permanently recorded.

Perhaps another one of these books that will be opened is the Book of the Law containing the righteous requirements of the law given from Mount Sinai and a record of all the times we have violated them. The Bible says that the law was given not to make us righteous but to shut our mouths so that we might see that we are guilty before God. So for those who claim to have kept the Ten Commandments, it will one day be obvious that even they fall short of God's standard—perfection.

Perhaps another one of these books will contain a record of every time we have heard the gospel. Wouldn't it be interesting to see a video playback of our lives?

> ACCORDING TO SCRIPTURE, EVERYTHING WE DO, EVERY WORD WE SPEAK, IS PERMANENTLY RECORDED.

There was a television show many years ago called *This Is Your Life*. The host would surprise a different famous participant each week, bringing together people out of that person's past—from favorite teachers to grade school friends. Imagine if God were to host a *This Is Your Life* episode in heaven, with everything we did flashed up there on a big screen—letter-box format. And there would be a record of every time we heard the gospel—as small children, in our teenage years, in adulthood. Judgment Day may actually be a lot like that. From Scripture, we know that one thing is certain. We will each be held accountable for how we responded to Jesus Christ.

Each of us has sinned. But the ultimate issue is the Son of God. What about him? Is Jesus Lord? Is he the Son of God? Did he die on the cross for the sins of humanity? Was he raised from the dead on the third day? Is he Savior and Lord or a fraud, a liar, or a lunatic?

C. S. Lewis said, "A man who was merely a man and said the sort of things that Jesus said wouldn't be a great moral teacher. He'd either be a lunatic . . . or else he'd be the devil of Hell." Each of us must make a choice: Either this man was, and is, the Son of God—or a madman or something worse.

"Wait," you might say. "I don't reject him. I admire him." But Jesus did not say, "Admire me." He said, "Follow me." And to be quite honest, I don't think he appreciates it when people classify him merely as a great humanitarian or moral teacher. He made claims that were very specific and exclusive. He claimed not only to be a messenger from God but God the messenger. He claimed to be God incarnate—a human being. And he claimed to be the only way to the Father. Now, was he right or wrong? That's what each individual must decide. The answer to that question—and nothing else—decides one's eternal fate.

So what's it going to be? Heaven or hell? Comfort or torment? Know this: God wants you in heaven! One day Jesus prayed to the his Father and said, "I desire that they may be with us and behold my glory." There you clearly see God's tender heart of love toward you. You see, when you're in love with someone, you want them with you. God is so in love with you that he poured out his wrath on his own dear Son so we wouldn't have to face it! Jesus came to pay a debt he did not owe because we owed a debt we could not pay!

Let's say you were driving down the freeway and you were on your way to cross a bridge over a raging river. Suddenly you saw a large sign emblazoned with the words Warning! Bridge Out! Use Other Exit! but you were determined, so you sped up toward that bridge. As you got closer, you saw more signs: Do Not Enter! Danger! Bridge Out! Still you sped on. Construction workers waved frantically at you, telling you to turn back. You sped by them, ignoring their warnings. As you got really close, you saw police cars with lights flashing and officers waving and yelling for you to turn back, yet still you sped on until you broke through those barriers and plunged over the side of that bridge to a watery grave. Now, whose fault was it that you died: the construction crew's? the police officers'? No, it was your fault. You ignored the warnings.

In the same way, people who end up in hell on that final day will have no one to blame but themselves. God has clearly placed warning signs. He has told us that "the wages of sin is death." If we end up in that dreadful place called hell, we will have no one to blame but ourselves. Again, to quote C. S. Lewis, "The gates of hell are locked from the inside."

WHAT DOES JESUS' CROSS MEAN TO ME?

CHAPTER 6

When it comes to the big questions of life, none is more important than the issue of the Crucifixion, for this was no mere historical event. Something incredibly profound took place two thousand years ago that even to-day has a direct effect upon our lives. Understanding the Crucifixion and its eternal significance will answer many of our spiritual questions.

Who would have ever thought it? Here we are in the beginning of the twenty-first century, and Jesus Christ is front and center. The Christian faith continues to thrive and flourish.

This, of course, comes as a great surprise to the pundits and critics out there who assured us of the certain demise of Christianity. You might be interested in knowing that these dire predictions of the disappearance of the Christian faith are not new. As far back as the times of the apostles there were those who thought they would personally eradicate Christianity.

One of the Roman emperors who persecuted the church was Diocletian. His attacks against the first-century Christians were so intense that the believers were forced to go underground. Diocletian was so confident that he would succeed that he actually had a coin struck with the words "The Christian religion is destroyed and the worship of the Roman gods is restored." Needless to say, that statement was certainly proved wrong. And where is Diocletian today? Virtually forgotten! Where is the Christian church today? Alive and well!

Some in the last century thought that the Christian faith would be long forgotten. Paul Johnson, in an article titled "The Real Message of the Millennium," wrote: "It was German philosopher Friedrich Neitzshe who started the 'God is dead' rumor in 1882. George Bernard Shaw and H. G. Wells fueled speculation by suggesting that the twentieth-century would mark the end of religious history. As late as the mid-1950s, Julian Huxley, the director-general of UNESCO, said that 'God is beginning to resemble not a ruler, but the last fading smile of a cosmic Cheshire cat.'" Yet here we are in a new century, and Christianity is alive and well, thank you. That is because the One we follow, Jesus Christ, is alive and well. Yes, it's been two thousand years since the birth of Jesus Christ, yet his life, death, and resurrection were and are, to this very day, so significant that we actually divide human time by them.

What is it about this man Jesus that so fascinates and mystifies people? Without question, he was the most extraordinary, influential, and yes, revolutionary person to stride the stage of human history. More books have been written about Jesus than about any other figure of the past. More music has been composed. More pictures have been painted. More drama has been written about him than about any other person. Why is this? Why does one single man occupy such a unique and unforgettable place in human history? Why doesn't his memory fade away like that of so many others who were significant in their time?

No other leader in history is even considered in the same breath as Jesus. Not Alexander the Great, Julius Caesar, George Washington, Abraham Lincoln, Napoleon, Ghandi. There is something about Jesus Christ that sets him apart from everyone else. Unlike all other leaders of the past, Jesus remains as much, if not more, of a focus of interest and influence in our society as contemporary leaders. Why? Because there has never, ever been anyone like Jesus. He was more than a prophet or a "great humanitarian." More than a "good man," he was the "God-man." Not man becoming a "god" (that's impossible) but God becoming a Man. And it all comes down to what happened on that crude wooden cross some two thousand years ago.

Tragically for many today the cross has become little more than a fashion accessory worn casually around the neck. It comes in gold or silver and is sometimes studded with pearls, diamonds, emeralds, rubies, or sapphires. But the cross that Jesus died upon centuries ago made no fashion statement. It was a crude wooden device designed by the Romans as a cheap and lethal torture rack.

Today some view the crucifixion of Jesus Christ as a rude interruption of what was just another wonderful life lived out on earth by a great humanitarian and moral teacher. But in Scripture we read that dying on the cross was the purpose of Jesus from the very beginning. His death was foreshadowed at the time of his birth when the wise men brought the unusual gifts of gold, frankincense, and myrrh. He was given gold because he was destined to be a king. He was presented with frankincense because he would stand as a high priest between sinful humanity and a holy, sinless God. Myrrh, however, was used as an embalming element in ancient Israel. It signified that Christ's mission here on earth was to redeem us by shedding his blood on the cross.

Long before Jesus' birth in Bethlehem, God had a plan for Jesus to come to earth to give humanity a second chance at a relationship with God. The Bible describes Jesus Christ as a Lamb slain from the foundation of the world—that's how long ago it was decided that he would die on a cross.

Jesus' death was also foreshadowed in the gripping tale of Abraham and his beloved son Isaac. God had blessed Abraham with a son in his old age. The aged man of God was so delighted by this young boy that he named him Isaac, which meant "laughter." Isaac brought joy and laughter into the home of Abraham and Sarah. So imagine what kind of shock it must have been when God came to Abraham one day and said, "Take now your son, your only son Isaac, whom you love . . . and offer him there as a burnt offering" (Genesis 22:2). There was no greater sacrifice that God could have asked of Abraham. Isaac was the light of his life. He meant everything to this man. But God asked him to give up his son. This is not only a story of obedience to God but an illustration of the magnitude of the sacrifice God would one day make for us at Calvary. "For God so loved the world that He gave His only begotten Son, that whoever believes in Him should not perish but have everlasting life" (John 3:16).

When Abraham took Isaac up to that place of sacrifice, his son said to him, "My father! . . . Where is the lamb for a burnt offering?" And Abraham said, "My son, God will provide for Himself the lamb for a burnt offering" (Genesis 22:7-8).

□ □ □ □ □

That is exactly what happened on the cross: God himself became the sacrifice when he gave his only Son whom he loved. Jesus was God incarnate.

The story of what happened at the Cross is one I never tire of telling. Jesus was betrayed by one of his own disciples and then arrested at the Garden of Gethsemane on trumped-up charges. The religious rulers were jealous of his popularity and angry at his ability to show what most of them really were— charlatans. They did not want to put Jesus to death themselves, so they tried to involve the Roman governor Pontius Pilate. Pilate did not want to deal with Jesus personally. He was extremely cautious in taking action against Jesus. Pilate's wife had had a dream about Jesus and warned her husband not to have anything to do with "that just man." Thus, Pilate wanted to wash his hands of this controversial case. When he heard that the Lord had spent time ministering in Galilee, he was relieved to have found a "loophole" and decided to reassign the trial to his longtime rival, Herod, who had jurisdiction over the region. Herod examined Jesus, mocked him, and sent him back. Now Pilate found himself on the horns of a dilemma. It appeared he would be forced to make a decision, and he continued to struggle to find a way out.

Pilate had Jesus scourged. This form of punishment was

incredibly cruel, employing a whip that had a short wooden handle with cords of leather embedded with bits of metal and bone. Every time the whip came down on the backs of prisoners, it would literally rip the flesh to shreds. No one was expected to be able to physically endure the entire forty lashes—minus one for mercy. Most criminals would quickly confess to whatever crime they had committed. But because Jesus had committed no crime, he had to withstand all thirty-nine lashes upon his back. This flogging ripped the flesh and skeletal tissue, sometimes leaving vital organs exposed. Then the beaten and bloodied Jesus was taken before the people, and Pilate said, "Behold the man," hoping that the sight of this sadistically treated individual would elicit sympathy from the bloodthirsty crowd. Instead, tragically, they yelled out in unison, "Let Him be crucified! . . . His blood be on us and on our children" (Matthew 27:23-25). At one point Pilate offered the people a choice between Jesus and Barabbas, a known insurrectionist and rebel against Rome. But to Pilate's chagrin, the people chose to spare Barabbas instead of Jesus (see Matthew 27:16-26).

> *Then the soldiers of the governor took Jesus into the Praetorium and gathered the whole garrison around Him. And they stripped Him and put a scarlet robe on Him. When they had twisted a crown of thorns, they put it on His head, and a reed in His right hand. And they bowed the knee before Him and mocked Him, saying, "Hail, King of the Jews!" Then they spat on Him, and took the reed and struck Him on the head. And when they had mocked Him, they took the robe off Him, put his own clothes on Him, and led Him*

away to be crucified. Now as they came out, they found a man of Cyrene, Simon by name. Him they compelled to bear His cross. And when they had come to a place called Golgotha, that is to say, Place of a Skull, they gave Him sour wine mingled with gall to drink. But when He had tasted it, He would not drink. Then they crucified Him, and divided His garments, casting lots, that it might be fulfilled which was spoken by the prophet: "They divided My garments among them, and for My clothing they cast lots." Sitting down, they kept watch over Him there. And they put up over His head the accusation written against Him: THIS IS JESUS THE KING OF THE JEWS. Then two robbers were crucified with Him, one on the right and another on the left. And those who passed by blasphemed Him, wagging their heads and saying, "You who destroy the temple and build it in three days, save Yourself! If You are the Son of God, come down from the cross." Likewise the chief priests also, mocking with the scribes and elders, said, "He saved others; Himself He cannot save. If He is the King if Israel, let Him now come down from the cross, and we will believe Him. He trusted in God; let Him deliver Him now if He will have Him; for He said, 'I am the Son of God.'" Even the robbers who were crucified with Him reviled Him with the same thing. (Matthew 27:27-44)

When we see cinematic or artistic renditions of the Crucifixion, we usually see a few stripes on Jesus' back with a little blood seeping through his robe. But that's not how it would have been. Jesus would have been badly beaten and very disfigured. An accurate cinematic portrayal would have to be rated R for extreme violence.

He was scourged. He was beaten about the face. His beard was ripped away. His face was swollen. As hard as these Roman soldiers were, it's impossible to imagine that they didn't have at least some sympathy for Jesus. But instead, as I referenced earlier, they pressed a crown of large thorns into his scalp, causing lacerations and profuse bleeding. They mocked him with this crown of thorns—this imitation of a real crown that a king would wear.

But in a way it was fitting. Thorns were a part of the curse that came upon humanity when Adam and Eve sinned in the Garden of Eden. This crown of thorns was symbolic of that curse. Jesus was, in effect, about to "curse the curse." Galatians 3:13 says, "Christ has redeemed us from the curse of the law, having become a curse for us (for it is written, 'Cursed is everyone who hangs on a tree')."

> AN ACCURATE CINEMATIC PORTRAYAL OF THE CRUCIFIXION WOULD HAVE TO BE RATED R FOR EXTREME VIOLENCE.

Then they took a reed, symbolic of the scepter that a king would hold, and they beat him with it. It was as if they were saying to him, "Well, King, where is your army? Where are your loyal subjects? Where are those who are here to defend you against all of us?"

By now a whole garrison of Roman troops had gathered

around Jesus. A garrison would number around six hundred. Imagine the scene in your mind: six hundred Roman troops in uniform forming a large circle around Jesus. They were the elite Legionnaires stationed in Jerusalem. To be stationed there was a prestigious assignment. These soldiers would have represented the cream of Rome's crop.

If only those Roman soldiers could have seen things as they really were. Surrounded by all of the soldiers, Jesus may have looked like the victim. But in the supernatural realm, there were hundreds—perhaps even thousands—of angels with swords drawn waiting for orders.

In the Garden of Gethsemane, Jesus said to Peter, who was trying to defend the Lord, "Do you think that I cannot now pray to My Father, and He will provide Me with more than twelve legions of angels?" (Matthew 26:53). *Legion* was a Roman term. A legion numbered around six thousand. If Jesus was speaking literally here, it meant that he had at his immediate disposal seventy-two thousand angels—all waiting for a word from him. From Scripture we know that angels are very powerful. In the Old Testament we read that one angel alone killed 185,000 enemies of Israel. Thus, seventy-two thousand angels could do considerable damage. Jesus had an army. It was his humility, and his destiny, that stopped him from calling upon them.

Without opposition, Jesus was led away meekly, beaten, bleeding, carrying the cross on which he was to be nailed and on which he would die an excruciatingly painful death. It's possible he carried only the crossbar, which would be attached to the large post that was placed in the ground. Then again, it's possible he was forced to carry the entire cross, which would have weighed nearly three hundred pounds. Think about that: three hundred pounds! To carry that much weight would be a tremendous feat for anyone, but Jesus had already been severely beaten. He had lost a considerable amount of blood. His untreated wounds throbbed mercilessly. Nevertheless, he was at least momentarily able to carry the cross.

At the place of crucifixion, the Bible tells us the Roman soldiers offered Jesus sour wine mingled with gall to drink. That may appear to be an act of mercy on the part of Rome to dull the pain. But in reality it was something the Romans did to stupefy a victim in order to minimize resistance to the crucifixion. Jesus, however, refused to drink the mixture, choosing instead to bear the full weight of what lay ahead.

Although the method of torture known as crucifixion originated in Persia, the Romans perfected it as a form of inexpensive capital punishment designed to produce slow death with maximum pain and suffering. It was one of the most disgraceful and cruel methods of execution—usually reserved only for slaves, foreign subversives, and the most hardened criminals. The Romans were responsible for crucifying thousands of people. It was not uncommon upon entering a Roman city to see the roads lined on both sides with crosses of crucified men standing as examples to anyone who would dare to defy the authority of Rome.

At Golgotha, Jesus was laid on the cross. His shredded back was placed upon it. The left foot was pressed backwards against the right foot, and a spike was driven through it.

Archaeologists recently discovered a crucified man dating to the time of Christ. They were able to determine that the spikes used in the Roman crucifixion were five to seven inches long, sharp at the front and then widening toward the back, according to John MacArthur in his commentary on the Gospel of Matthew.

Dr. Truman Davis gave this description of what took place at the Crucifixion in an article entitled "The Crucifixion of Jesus from a Medical Point of View":

As the arms fatigue, great waves of cramps sweep over the muscles knotting them in deep relentless throbbing pain. When these cramps come, there is the inability to push himself upward, so hanging by his arms the pectoral muscles are paralyzed and the intercostal muscles are unable to act. Air can be drawn into the lungs but it cannot be exhaled. So Jesus fights to raise himself in order to get one short breath. Finally carbon dioxide builds up in the lungs and in the bloodstream and the cramps partially subside. Spasmodically he is able to push himself upward to exhale and bring in life giving oxygen. Hours of this limitless pain, cycles of twisting, joint-rending cramps, intermittent partial asphyxiation, searing pain as tissue is torn from his lacerated back as he pushes up and down against the rough timber. A deep crushing pain in the chest as the heart fills with serum and begins to compress, it is almost over. The compressed heart is struggling to pump heavy, thick, sluggish blood into the tissue. The tortured lungs are making a frantic effort to gasp in small gulps of air.

It's a tragic picture of what Jesus was going through on the cross. But the worst was yet to come, for the sin of the world was about to be poured out on him.

◻ ◻ ◻ ◻ ◻

Matthew tells us that there were two robbers crucified with Jesus on that day. These were not petty thieves or common robbers. These were men who plundered as they stole—cruel bandits who took pleasure in tormenting, abusing, and often killing their victims. They were the worst of the worst—the lowest of the low. And they were crucified on each side of Jesus.

In spite of the fact that they, too, were facing death, they joined the crowd in saying, "You who destroy the temple and build it in three days, save Yourself. If You are the Son of God, come down from the cross" (Matthew 27:40). This, of course, was a misinterpretation of something Jesus had stated about Herod's temple: "Not one stone shall be left here upon another" (Matthew 24:2). He had also said, speaking of his own body, "Destroy this temple, and in three days I will raise it up" (John 2:19). Some of the crowd apparently misunderstood these statements to mean that Jesus was planning to destroy the temple of Herod. That was never the case. Instead, he was saying, "You destroy this body of mine, and in three days I will rise from the dead."

In Matthew's account, we read that both criminals joined in with the taunting crowd. Luke's Gospel, however, expands on this story and relates that one of the criminals turned to Jesus and said, "Lord, remember me when You come into Your kingdom" (Luke 23:42). Some have even suggested that this represents an apparent contradiction in the Bible. But that is not the case. It is simply an illustration of why God gave us four Gospels—four witnesses to these events. Each brings a different perspective of what took place. This thief did actually join in with the others present at the cross, saying, "Save Yourself" (Matthew 27:40). But when Jesus said, "Father, forgive them, for they do not know what they do" (Luke 23:34), it must have been as a lightening bolt striking this thief's hardened heart. Suddenly in a moment, in a flash, he realized that Jesus *was*

> THE SPIKES USED IN THE ROMAN CRUCIFIXION WERE FIVE TO SEVEN INCHES LONG, SHARP AT THE FRONT AND THEN WIDENING TOWARD THE BACK.

the Son of God. Something deeply touched this man, and he believed.

Conversion can happen just that quickly. It's worth noting that both of these criminals had the opportunity to become believers through the witness of Jesus on the cross. But the Scripture tells us that one believed and one did not. Isn't that indicative of the mystery of the gospel? Whenever it is proclaimed, some hear—and some do not. Some believe—and some do not.

"Lord, remember me when you come into your kingdom," one of the criminals said to Jesus.

"Assuredly, I say to you, today you will be with Me in Paradise" (Luke 23:43), Jesus answered him.

Talk about being in the right place at the right time! This

criminal was facing eternal separation from God, but he managed to be crucified next to God incarnate who pardoned him on the spot—absolved of all sin.

But that was one of the few bright spots on that day of crucifixion. Where were Jesus' other champions? Where was Peter? Where were those he had healed? Where were all those whose lives he had touched? Mostly, Jesus faced hatred and ridicule that fateful day.

Someone else was present that day who had the opportunity to give the Lord some support. A Cyrenian named Simon, the Bible says, was compelled to carry the cross for Jesus when he was unable to bear the weight. Simon wasn't from Jerusalem. He was a visitor. Scripture does not record why he was in town. Maybe he was there for Passover. Maybe he just saw all the commotion and walked over to see what was going on. But this man was given one of the greatest privileges afforded to anyone in human history. He was selected to carry the cross of Jesus—chosen for a few moments in history to carry the Lord's cross and reduce his pain and suffering for a time.

We have this privilege today. Jesus said, "If anyone desires to come after Me, let him deny himself, and take up his cross, and follow Me. For whoever desires to save his life will lose it, and whoever loses his life for My sake will find it" (Matthew 16:24-25). Jesus is still looking for men and women like Simon to pick up the cross and carry it.

People talk about the various crosses they are forced to bear. Some say, "My cross in life is my children. They are a cross to bear." And their children probably say, "My cross in life is my parents." The cross is not one particular troubling problem. The cross is the same for every person. If we had been alive two thousand years ago and had seen Jesus walking through the city bearing his cross, we would have automatically known he was going to his execution. A person who carried a cross in ancient Israel was always on his way to die.

So when Jesus says, "Take up the cross," what is he saying? To take up the cross, or to bear the cross, means to place our will in subordination to his Word. It means to be willing to die to our own ambition, our own plans, our own choices. When our will and desires do not conflict with Scripture, God will allow us to follow our own choices. Yet our choices must at all times be subject to and not in conflict with the Scriptures. To take up his cross is to stand up for him—even when it is not popular. It means to be willing to take God's will above our own.

> TO TAKE UP THE CROSS, OR TO BEAR THE CROSS, MEANS TO PLACE OUR WILL IN SUBORDINATION TO HIS WORD.

Taking up the cross means to follow and obey his Word. It means to love God more than anyone or anything else. It means to love our neighbors as we love ourselves. It means being willing to make sacrifices if he asks us to do so. It also means living life to the fullest.

Do you want to find out what life is all about? First, stop being so obsessed with self. Jesus did not say, "Esteem yourself." He said, "Deny yourself." In so doing, you will "find yourself."

Because we live in a culture that is so obsessed with self, I know it sounds contradictory when God says, "Forget about yourself. Stop whining. Take up your cross, and you will find life." But you must first die to self.

How is that? When we put God's will above our own, we discover that his plans for us are better than our plans for ourselves. When we put God's purposes above our own, we find out that he loves us and cares for us and is looking out for our eternal benefit.

How do we respond to Jesus as Savior, who laid down his life for us, who shed his blood for us, who died for us? The question is, Will we live for him?

It was because of what Jesus did for us on the cross that we can now have a relationship with God Almighty. If there was any other way to deal with the horrible sinfulness of humanity, God would have found it. But there wasn't. Only the death of his Son, Jesus Christ, could satisfy God's requirement of righteousness. God the Father poured all the collective sin of the world upon his own dear Son that dark day two thousand years ago. Today it's the greatest insult to God when someone says, "I don't need to approach God through Jesus. I'll go my own way."

If it were possible for us to approach God on our own, it would not have been necessary for Jesus to die on the cross. The Bible asks the question, "How shall we escape if we neglect so great a salvation?" (Hebrews 2:3).

□ □ □ □ □

Imagine for a moment that you're in the courtroom of life. Before you sits the Judge. On your left sits the man accusing you, the prosecuting attorney. On your right sits your court-appointed Attorney.

As you stand before the Judge, you feel as though the eyes of all humanity are upon you. You feel a slight twinge in your stomach. You never thought you would be in this situation—on trial for all you have done with your life. In your mind you did fairly well. You were generally respectful of others, tried to help people when you could, never committed any really serious offenses against society. Nevertheless, as you stand in front of the Judge, you notice a sign behind him that reads: The Penalty for Sin Is Death! All Violators Will Be Prosecuted.

Try as you might, you can't quite get a glimpse of the Judge's face, but his robes are a brilliant white. When he says, "Court is now in session," a hushed awe fills the court. You feel unprepared.

Your Attorney, Jesus, doesn't seem overly concerned with your troubles. He sits patiently at the table, his eyes fixed on the Judge.

First to approach the bench is the prosecuting attorney. His name is Satan. He's tall, dark, and handsome. His clothes are the finest you've ever seen. He has a winning smile and a confident stride that portend cockiness. Before moving all the way to the bench, he stops to give you a once-over. You detect a slight smile at the corner of his lips, and his eyes reveal a sinister hatred. You think to yourself, *He's actually enjoying this!* The knot in your stomach grows tighter.

In a rich baritone voice he says, "Your Honor, before you today is someone who in no way measures up to the standards you have set for humanity. You yourself have said, 'Be perfect, just as your Father in heaven is perfect' (Matthew 5:48). You know this person has fallen short of that mark. To support my case, allow me to recall the sins this person has committed."

With that he begins rattling off a list of your failures. They are not great sins—most of them can be explained. He recounts things like selfishness, greed, gossip, lies, some cheating (at a small level), evil thoughts, fits of anger. But then he starts pulling up things from the past that you don't even remember. As he reads down his list, the minutes turn into hours, then days, then weeks—and he's still not finished! Your stomach sinks as you realize that you're in serious trouble. You look over at your Defense Attorney, but he doesn't appear to be all that concerned.

You think, *Jesus, what are you doing? Can't you stand up and say something on my behalf?* Yet Jesus just sits there, almost as if he knows something you don't know.

Finally, Satan reaches the end of his lengthy list and says, "As we all know, this person has broken the law. You have said, 'Whoever shall keep the whole law, and yet stumble in one point, he is guilty of all' (James 2:10). Obviously, this person deserves judgment and death." At last he sits down with a smug and contented look on his face, knowing he has nailed you to the wall.

At this point your Defense Attorney stands up and asks the Judge for permission to approach the bench. Jesus then slowly steps forward, and with his first word changes your whole outlook on these proceedings. He says to the Judge, "Father, we both know this person has done everything the devil has said. But we also know that you sent me—your only Son—to pay the penalty for that sin. That I have done, and so I ask you to forgive this client on my behalf."

"You're right," says the Judge. With that he looks at Satan and says, "Case dismissed. All is forgiven." He pounds his gavel down to emphasize the finality of that statement.

☐ ☐ ☐ ☐ ☐

Have you ever wondered what your defense will be when you stand before God?

There is a legal proverb that says, "He who is his own lawyer has a fool for a client." You will fail miserably if you try to plead your own case before God. If you want Jesus to represent you in the courtroom of life, you must come to the end of yourself, realizing your inability to make it on your own, recognizing your need for a Savior.

There is just one lifeline thrown to earth from heaven. Jesus is that lifeline.

WHY DO I FEEL GUILTY?

CHAPTER 7

In his excellent book The Vanishing Conscience, *John MacArthur points out some interesting modern illustrations of the growing unpopularity of guilt.*[1]

Remember the story of Kathryn Powers, the fugitive from justice who placed herself in the hands of authorities after twenty-three years? She had been involved with a radical group back in the seventies and had participated in a bank robbery in which a police officer, the father of nine children, was shot in the back and killed. For fourteen years, Kathryn Powers was on the FBI's most-wanted list. In a much-publicized decision to confess and put the past behind her, Powers turned herself in.

When she was asked what motivated her to do so, she said, "Back then I was naïve and unthinking." About her surrender, she explained, "I know I must answer this accusation from the past in order to live with a full authenticity in the present." Her husband added, "She did not return out of guilt. She wanted to be whole."[2]

To this, I would have to ask, What's wrong with a little

guilt? Shouldn't someone feel guilty about committing such a crime? Is guilt such a bad thing?

San Francisco supervisor Dan White murdered another supervisor, Harvey Milk, as well as the mayor of San Francisco, George Moscone. He said he did it because he ate too much junk food, especially Hostess Twinkies. A lenient jury found him guilty of voluntary manslaughter rather than double murder. Whatever happened to guilt? What about taking personal responsibility? Even if those powerful Twinkies had some mysterious effect on his state of mind, wouldn't you expect Dan White would feel some guilt—some expression of remorse—over the death of his colleagues?[3]

Then there was the case of a burglar who was shot and paralyzed while committing a crime in New York. His attorney told the jury that the burglar was a victim of society, driven to crime by socioeconomic disadvantages. He actually was awarded millions in financial compensation from the city and the police officer who shot him. Once again, whatever happened to guilt?[4]

It seems that whenever we turn on the television these days, courtroom dramas are playing out before our eyes. We hear about two brothers who killed their parents. Their defense? They claimed they were victims of years of abuse and that they were driven to commit the double murder.[5]

No one wants to be held responsible for anything anymore. Consequently, there is no such thing as guilt. Everybody's a victim. That's the new rationalization for crime and misdeeds—behavior the Bible calls sin. Some syndrome or disorder or past-life experience drove us to it. We have learned to say we can't help ourselves.

Anyone who scoffs at this terminology is charged as insensitive—politically incorrect! It seems our culture has declared war on guilt. The very concept of guilt is considered outdated, backward, even hurtful. Those troubled by guilt are referred to therapists, who take it upon themselves to boost that person's self-image. It is ironic that our society encourages sin, then explains away the guilt that sin produces.

In his book *A Nation of Victims,* Charles Sikes writes: "The politics of victimization have taken the place of more traditional expressions of morality and equity. If you lose a job, you can sue for the mental distress of being fired. If your bank goes broke, the government will insure your deposit. If you drive drunk and crash, you can sue someone for failing to warn you to stop drinking. There is always someone else to blame. No one is guilty anymore."[6]

Ann Landers, who has a widely read column in newspapers across the United States, made this statement about guilt: "One of the most painful self-mutilating time- and energy-consuming exercises in the human experience is guilt. It can ruin your day, your week, or your whole life if you let it." She concludes, "Remember, guilt is a pollutant, and we don't need any more of it in the world."[7]

Is that true? Is guilt a pollutant? Or is there a need for it? If you ask me, I think we could use some more guilt in our society. Guilt has its place. It does serve a purpose.

It reminds me of a story about a practical joke played many years ago by Sir Arthur Conan Doyle, author of the Sherlock Holmes series. One day Doyle, as a joke, jotted off a note to twelve of his friends. On this note he simply wrote these words: "Flee at once. All is discovered."

Within twenty-four hours, all twelve of his friends had left the country! That's a guilty conscience for you!

Granted, psychological studies have shown that false guilt can be counterproductive to a person's ability to live effectively. False guilt can paralyze a person from partaking in life to the fullest. But the false guilt that produces constant condemnation in a person's life and the kind that appropriately convicts our conscience are two different things entirely. False condemnation is a by-product of the devil's constant accusations before the Father. One of Satan's personas is "the accuser of the brethren." According to the Bible, he stands day and night before God, bringing accusation against believers in an effort to paralyze Christians from effective living by heaping upon them condemnation. He may constantly remind us of our past: "You're no good! How could God ever forgive you for that? Why should you have any credibility as a Christian? Why should anyone ever listen to you? After all, you once did such and such . . . !" The Bible says, "There is therefore now no condemnation to those who are in Christ Jesus" (Romans 8:1). Condemnation is one thing, and we don't have to put up with that. Conscience produced by twinges of guilt when we have done—or are about to do— something wrong is another thing entirely. In that case, guilt is good: It keeps us out of trouble and on target.

Look at our country as it is today; it's in such a mess. In many ways we have defied God. We have done everything we can to remove him and his influence from our culture. We have

> IS GUILT A POLLUTANT? OR IS THERE A NEED FOR IT?

taken him out of our classrooms. We have taken him out of our courtrooms. We have taken him out of our culture as a whole.

Much of this was accomplished back in the sixties. My generation pushed away the boundaries and said, "We are going to find our own way. We are going to do what we want to do." What we vowed in the sixties, we are reaping now. We are reaping the results of our sin and abandoning God.

The Old Testament prophet Hosea warned that those who sow the wind will reap the whirlwind (see Hosea 8:7). In the sixties we laughed at the idea of values. We viewed the traditional family—with a father and a mother who remained faithful to each other for life—as antiquated and out of date. Yet, the majority of the problems facing our country today can be directly traced back to the breakdown of the family. We have forgotten God.

We must return to the foundation of biblical values and beliefs. We cannot sit idly by and continue to watch as the traditional family completely disintegrates. We have enough young people from broken homes searching for answers. We find them joining gangs. We find them getting into drugs. We find them choosing a lifestyle of violence. We are a nation under siege from our own children. Mothers are shot dead while they sit with their toddlers at bus stops. Young children are killed in their own homes when bullets fired in neighborhood drug disputes go through the walls of their apartments. Teenagers kill each other in school corridors over an insult or because someone wants somebody else's jacket or pair of shoes.

If we make choices that are contrary to God's laws, we must live with the consequences of what we choose—including the guilt that inevitably follows when we break God's laws.

□ □ □ □ □

One afternoon I was in my backyard. We saw this brightly colored little finch just sitting on the grass. You don't usually see those birds flying around because they are usually kept in cages as pets. I walked over to him gingerly, thinking he was going to quickly flutter away. Much to my surprise, this little bird just sat there. So I reached down and picked him up. This little finch perched on my finger. I said to my wife, Cathe, "Look at this little bird." She said, "Maybe he's scared." I said, "I don't know. He just sits there. Is this normal?" We were trying to bring this bird back to life and cheer him up. He just sat there, looking half-dead. We didn't know what to do with him. So we sent our son Jonathan down the street to a friend's house to get a birdcage. He brought the cage back, and as soon as we opened the cage and put him in, the little bird came to life. He perked up. He began chirping. He appeared to be instantly happy. I thought, "That's weird! You put a bird in a cage, and he's happy."

But apparently that cage did not represent prison to the bird—it represented protection. While some might see bars as confining and restrictive, this little bird saw bars as a means to keep away his predators.

In the same way God wants to protect us. That's why he gave us laws—parameters. That's why he said, "Don't be sexually active until you are married; then stay faithful to your spouse." That's why he said, "Don't lie. Don't steal. Don't kill." He did not give us laws in order to make our life miserable. He gave us laws in order to protect us—because he loves us. We sin when we break God's laws, and sin always produces guilt.

What does the Bible say about guilt? Romans 3:10-25 states:

"There is none righteous, no, not one; there is none who understands; there is none who seeks after God. They have all turned aside; they have together become improfitable; there is none who does good, no, not one." "Their throat is an open tomb; with their tongues they have practiced deceit"; "the poison of asps is under their lips"; "whose mouth is full of cursing and bitterness." "Their feet are swift to shed blood; destruction and misery are in their ways; and the way of peace they have not known." "There is no fear of God before their eyes." Now we know that whatever the law says, it says to those who are under the law, that every mouth may be stopped, and all the world may become guilty before God. Therefore by the deeds of the law no flesh will be justified in His sight, for by the law is the knowledge of sin. But now the righteousness of God apart from the law is revealed, being witnessed by the Law and the Prophets, even the righteousness of God, through faith in Jesus Christ, to all and on all who also believe. For there is no difference; for all have sinned and fall short of the glory of God, being justified freely by His grace through the redemption that is in Christ Jesus, whom God set forth as a propitiation by His blood, through faith, to demonstrate His righteousness, because in His forbearance God had passed over the sins that were previously committed.

These verses contain the answer to our guilt.

□ □ □ □ □

Why do people feel guilty? Because they *are* guilty. I didn't say that, the Bible did. We are all guilty. The guilt feelings we experience are the result of the real problem—our sin. And all the psychological counseling in the world cannot relieve us of our guilt due to sin. We can pretend it is not there. We can try to find someone else to blame for our problems. But the only effective way to remove our guilt is to get to the root of the problem—our sin.

In this passage from Romans the apostle Paul is showing that every person is guilty before God—the religious person as well as the unbelieving pagan. Everyone is guilty of failing to meet God's standard of righteousness.

Imagine yourself in a court of law standing before God, as in the previous chapter. You are being tried for not having lived up to his righteous standards. Although you realize you have fallen short, you feel that you have done some good things as well—some good deeds that should be noted. So you are hoping that those good deeds will be brought before the Judge in your defense to demonstrate to him that you are not such a bad person after all.

Paul is showing us why this line of defense will not work in God's court. He uses testimony from God's Word, and no one escapes the charges.

First, Paul deals with our character in Romans, chapter 3: "There is none righteous, no, not one." Then he says, "There is none who does good, no, not one."

What does this mean? That there is no good person walking the face of the earth today? We all know some good people who aren't Christians—genuinely nice, considerate people. We have met people who are not Christians who are honest and sincerely concerned about others. We might even say they are good people. Is the Bible saying this is not true?

Let's understand what Paul is really saying here. He does not mean that there aren't men and women who do commendable things. This verse is not saying that there are no humanitarians or that there are no genuine heroes.

To say there is "none who does good, no, not one," does not mean that there are not good things that we can do. It means there is no good in us that can satisfy God. When the Bible says there is "none righteous, no, not one," it means none of us is as good as God requires. None of us measures up to God's standards.

What are God's standards? Well, they are pretty high. Absolute, flawless perfection—that is the standard, and it pretty much ruins it for all of us. No mistakes, no sins. No one is that good, and no one is that righteous. In other words, a person who is not as good as God is not acceptable to God.

Let's say a group of us all decided we were going to jump up and touch the moon. So you ran and took a flying leap and managed to jump eight feet into the air. Not bad. Then I ran and jumped and only got up to four feet—not as good as you but better than nothing. Let's say one of our friends was an Olympic pole vaulter who ran as fast as his muscular legs could carry him, firmly planted his pole, and flung himself thirty feet closer to the moon than you or I. Very impressive!

But did any of us even get remotely close to our goal of

jumping as high as the moon? No. It's the same when people say they can meet God's standards and get into heaven by their good deeds or morality. The intent may be honorable, but the results fall pitifully short of the mark. Without doubt, some people are more moral than others. Some live exemplary lives in many ways. But each of us falls miserably short of God's high standards. We keep hitting that massive, impeding wall called sin.

This may come as a shock, but human beings are capable of incredible wickedness. We all are. The potential for wickedness is there. We may on occasion do good things. But there is wickedness deep inside us. We meet people all the time who say, "I'm on a spiritual journey. I am searching for the truth. I'm trying to find the light. I'm trying to find God."

God plainly declares in Jeremiah 29:13, "You will seek Me and find Me, when you search for Me with all your heart." Let me be very blunt. Those who are seeking God will eventually find their way to Jesus Christ. If not, they may not really be seeking God after all, but just playing religious games. They may be dabbling with different belief systems. But true seekers will find the one true God. Why? Because religion is man's search for God. But Christianity is *God's search for man*.

Sometimes we hear people say, "I found the Lord ten years ago." It sounds like God was lost.

As I understand the Bible, God wasn't lost; we were. He was seeking to save us. If we really want to know him, we will find him. Many simply never come to Jesus Christ because they bristle at the thought of having to admit their sinfulness. They are unwilling to accept God's assessment of them. They are unwilling to acknowledge their guilt. The idea of guilt irritates them. They want to believe they can get to heaven through their own merit, their own goodness, their own deeds. But the Bible says that isn't possible. All people need a Savior from their sin. No one is exempt from this truth.

The Bible says we are dead in trespasses and sin. That's important to understand because, among other things, the word *sin* means "to miss the mark." We have missed God's mark of perfection. We have not measured up to his expectations of us. But the word *trespass* means "to deliberately cross a line." Not only have we not measured up to God's demands, but we have crossed that line repeatedly. In fact, the Bible says: "All we like sheep have gone astray; we have turned, every one, to his own way" (Isaiah 53:6).

In the book of Genesis, the first book of the Old Testament, we find sinful man hiding among the trees. In Malachi, the last book of the Old Testament, God declares, "You have departed from the way." The Bible records a long history of humanity turning away from God—deliberately crossing the line, intentionally deserting him.

> EACH OF US FALLS MISERABLY SHORT OF GOD'S HIGH STANDARDS. WE KEEP HITTING THAT MASSIVE, IMPEDING WALL CALLED SIN.

Humankind has deliberately and repeatedly turned away from the offer of eternal life. If we wind up facing judgment, we will have no one to blame but ourselves because not only did we reject the offer of Jesus Christ to forgive us of our sin, but we practically had to climb over him to get into hell.

□ □ □ □ □

Finally, Paul addresses our conduct—what we do. "There is no fear of God" (Romans 3:18). Not only could we use a good dose of old-fashioned guilt in this day and age, we could use more fear and respect of God once again in our culture.

Psalm 111:10 tells us that "the fear of the Lord is the beginning of wisdom." When the Scripture speaks of fearing God, it doesn't mean that we are to cower and cringe before him. It is a word that speaks of reverence, awe, respect. It has been defined as a wholesome dread of displeasing him. To some of us, God has been misrepresented as a sort of angry demagogue—a "celestial killjoy" throwing bolts of lightning down from heaven on those who displeased him. This idea came from what is often called "hellfire and brimstone" preaching.

But that doesn't seem to be the problem anymore. When is the last time you heard a preacher even mention hell, much less preach on it?

I hear messages about how to be successful. I hear messages about positive and possibility thinking. I hear messages about how God will prosper me. But I rarely hear a sermon about a holy God who wants me to repent of my sin and walk with him. That's not a popular concept anymore.

Instead, we have been trying to develop a new God—an all-loving benign blob hovering up there in the universe. And his philosophy in life is, "I'm okay. You're okay. Whatever."

That's not the God of the Bible. The real God is without question a God of love. The real God loves you deeply. The real God is also holy. So not only should I love God but I should fear him. I should reverence him. I should stand in awe of him.

People say, "God accepts me as I am." Yes, he does. He loves you, but he wants you to change. Let's take this idea a step further: God wants you to change but also realizes that you cannot change on your own. You will need his help to change. In other words, God will accept you as you are, then lead you through changes as he brings his Word to bear upon your life, redirecting it according to his perfect plans for you.

God has a plan for our lives—but we can't achieve those plans without his help and direction.

Romans 3:19 says: "The law says . . . that every mouth may be stopped."

> WE HAVE BEEN TRYING TO DEVELOP A NEW GOD—AN ALL-LOVING BENIGN BLOB HOVERING UP THERE IN THE UNIVERSE. AND HIS PHILOSOPHY IN LIFE IS, "I'M OKAY. YOU'RE OKAY. WHATEVER."

Let me paraphrase: God gave the Ten Commandments to show us that we actually have nothing to boast about. Every one of us has broken these commandments. Romans 3:20 says, "By the deeds of the law no flesh will be justified." The law is a moral mirror.

It condemns but does not convert. It challenges but does not change. It points the finger but does not give mercy.

The law is a preparation for the gospel—the provision. Essentially, the law chases us into the open arms of Jesus. We look at the law and then look at God's standards and say, "I can't do that. I need help." And the Lord says, "That's why I am here." So we run into his open arms. He gives us the strength to change.

I admit this message sounds bleak. But it's the truth. Before we can appreciate the remedy or the cure, we must first understand the problem. If we don't realize we have a problem, we will never find the cure.

I don't like to go to the doctor. I imagine that's true for most of us. Going to the doctor is sort of an admission of defeat. I will fight sickness as long as I can. Finally, I will drag my miserable carcass over to the doctor's office and find out what I need to do to get well.

Think of Jesus as the Great Physician. The Doctor is always in. He is not out playing golf somewhere. He is always able to see me. I don't have to page him, nor will I get his voice mail when I call him. Thank God, when I have a crisis, I don't have to phone heaven and hear, "Hello—this is heaven. God is not in right now. Please press #1 if you need forgiveness . . . #2 if you need strength . . . #3 if you need direction." No, when I walk into his office, he will step right over to me and assess the situation. Then he'll say, "I've got some good news and some bad news. Here is the bad news." Then he assesses my condition. He tells me what is wrong with me. That's not pleasant. I don't enjoy that part of the process. I don't like hearing what he has to say about me. But I need to know it so I can appreciate the cure that he is about to prescribe.

So here it is. I'm not good. I have sinned. I feel guilt because I am guilty. I don't need to find myself. My *self* is the problem. Nor is the root of my problem a lack of self-esteem. According to the Bible, I am a sinner in need of a Savior.

Getting in touch with my inner child won't save me. Before I can be accepted, I must first accept my guilt.

So how do I get rid of this guilt? How can I be forgiven of my sin? How can I put my past behind me? Can I do some good deeds to counteract the bad deeds that I have done? Can I somehow atone for my sin? What can I do? Absolutely nothing!

It's not what I can do for God: It's what God has done for me.

Accepting that truth is the only way to find relief from guilt—the only way to find the forgiveness of sin. It's the only way to come into a relationship with God "that we might be justified by faith" (Galatians 3:24).

□   □   □   □   □

Now we come to three key words in Christian theology: *justification, redemption,* and *propitiation.* These may seem like big words, but they pack a lot of meaning. The Bible says that when I come to Christ and ask him to forgive me of my sin, I have been justified. What does that mean? It is a word that declares the "rightness" of something—not symbolically, not potentially, but actually. What has it done? One way to understand the word *justification* is to read it as, "just as if I had never sinned." I come to Christ. In faith, I ask his forgiveness. He says, "You are justified by your faith." That's incredible to think about, because guilt from our past sins can plague us. The devil can say, "You remember what you did. You remember this sin you committed twenty-three years ago?" And we can say, "I am justified—just as if I had never sinned." Only God can do that because of Jesus' work on the cross. God himself says, "Their sins and their lawless deeds I will remember no more" (Hebrews 10:17). "As far as the east is from the west, so far has He removed our transgressions from us" (Psalm 103:12). That's a long way off.

Or as Corrie ten Boom used to say, "God has taken our sin and thrown it into the sea of forgetfulness and posted a sign that says, 'No fishing allowed.'"

Why? Because of redemption. What does that mean? The word *redemption* carries the idea of purchasing something—paying a price. It was commonly used to describe paying a ransom to free a prisoner. Only a century and a half ago (or less) this was going on in our own country. People were sold on the auction block as slaves. Shackled prisoners would stand before a crowd, and people in the audience would bid on them, the slaves eventually going to those who were willing to pay the highest prices.

Picture yourself bound in shackles, standing in humiliation before a crowd of raucous bidders; there you stand, shivering, ashamed, frightened, unable to help yourself. Then Jesus walks boldly through the crowd, refusing to stop until he's right there beside you. He reaches down and unlocks your shackles, then says to the slavemaster, "This one is mine! I've already paid the price!" Finally, he whispers in your ear: "You're free!"

Wouldn't you be grateful if someone did something as unselfish as that for you? Wouldn't you want to do something in return? Since you cannot pay for that which is so valuable that it cannot be fixed with a price, there is just one thing to do. Voluntarily serve the One who freed you.

Jesus did even more than that when he offered himself in

my place. He paid the price and offered me propitiation. This word *propitiation* means "appeasement or satisfaction." When Jesus hung on the cross and cried out the words "It is finished!" (John 19:30), God's requirements for righteousness were satisfied. God was pleased, not with the horrendous suffering that Jesus faced, but what it accomplished. There was no other way to resolve the sin issue. The requirements for righteousness and for perfectly keeping the law were now met for all time.

The Bible tells us that sin is the problem we all face. Sin is the wall we keep running into throughout our lives. This wall of sin keeps us from God.

We are born with a nature to do wrong. Jeremiah 17:9 says: "The heart is deceitful above all things, and desperately wicked." That is why it is inconceivable that some people say, "The answer is within. Look deep within, and you will find all the answers of life. You are your own god. You have the truth." Looking deep within ourselves, we will simply discover that the problem—not the solution—is within. We will only find the solution when we seek beyond ourselves.

> FOR THOSE WHO BELIEVE THAT HUMANITY IS BASICALLY GOOD, IT MUST BE DIFFICULT TO EXPLAIN WHAT'S GOING ON IN THE WORLD TODAY.

For those who believe that humanity is basically good, it must be difficult to explain what's going on in the world today. The Nazis killed six million Jews and some twelve million people in total. Communism was responsible for even more death and destruction in its seventy-five-year history. It's amazing how wicked humans can be and the depths to which we are capable of sinking.

It comes back to the sin nature—the nature with which we were born—beginning in the Garden of Eden. Adam was given free will to choose right or wrong—total freedom to obey or disobey God's commands. He made the wrong choice. He rejected God's way and chose his own way.

Many of the problems in today's culture can be directly traced to our refusal to live God's way. We disobey his commandments. In many instances, we have forgotten them, perverted them, disregarded them. He gave us guidelines to help us live healthy and productive lives. Yet, we commit adultery. We kill. We steal. We lie. We do whatever we want if we think it will advance our own short-term interests.

It's all the result of what Adam did. The Bible says in Romans 5:18: "Therefore . . . as through one man's offense judgment came to all men, resulting in condemnation. . . ." Romans 5:12 says: "Through one man sin entered the world, and death through sin, and thus death spread to all men, because all sinned."

So be careful about pointing an accusing finger at the Creator and saying he has somehow botched up because society is falling apart at the seams. Because of our rejection of the standards given to us by the Creator, we have these many social problems.

The history of the human race from Adam's day to the present has been the story of man's futile efforts to gain back the position lost in Adam's fall.

Maybe you think, *Well, that's not fair. Adam did it. I*

didn't do it. Why should I suffer because of what somebody else did? But just think about it. If you or I had been in the Garden of Eden, we would have done the same thing. To prove that, just realize that every single day we are presented with hundreds—perhaps thousands—of choices between right or wrong, good or evil.

Faced with those choices, do we ever choose wrong? Of course we do. There is not a single day that the same test set before Adam is not presented to you and me.

The same two paths that God set before Adam have been set before us today—and we are still free to choose.

In Deuteronomy 30:19 God says, "I call heaven and earth as witnesses today against you, that I have set before you life and death, blessing and cursing; therefore choose life, that both you and your descendants may live." Each of us has that choice—life or death, good or evil, blessings or curses. We continue to choose to disobey God. As a result, we reap the miserable consequences. Because we are selfish, because we are prejudiced, because we have wicked hearts, we do the things we do—not because God has botched up. No, we can't blame God. The fault lies with us.

☐ ☐ ☐ ☐ ☐

Would you believe me if I told you I had discovered a new diet where we could eat only fattening foods and lose weight? The diet would consist of banana splits, pizza, coconut cream pies, doughnuts, fudge—you name it. Would you believe me?

What if I told you that I had found a new alcohol-recovery program where we were advised to drink a quart of Scotch every hour? Or what if I told you about a new way to get in shape by sitting in front of the television set, clicking away on your remote control? What if I told you that I had found a new way to get ahead in school by goofing off and playing video games?

We know none of these ridiculous suggestions will work. Why? Because if we eat fattening foods, we will get fat. If we drink constantly, we will become an alcoholic. If we sit around and do nothing, we will be out of shape. And if we don't study, we will flunk. Why? Because we reap what we sow.

We all know that there are certain laws that govern the universe. The law of thermodynamics says everything is expanding. The law of gravity says whatever goes up must come down. The law of Murphy says that anything that *can* go wrong... *will*. Well, okay—maybe Murphy's Law is not all that scientific, but it often seems so.

Then there is a law written in Galatians 6:7-8: "Do not be deceived, God is not mocked; for whatever a man sows, that he will also reap. For he who sows to his flesh will of the flesh reap corruption, but he who sows to the Spirit will of the Spirit reap everlasting life."

If you want to achieve certain goals in life, then you must do what it takes to reach them. And if you want to avoid certain consequences, you must avoid doing anything that would lead to negative or tragic results.

The Bible gives us this truth—and it doesn't change, regardless of who you are. If you say, "I don't believe in the law of gravity" and jump off a building, you will hit the pavement just as hard as the true believer in that unchanging law. If you say, "I don't believe in the principle of sowing and reaping," you will still reap what you sow.

The Bible says: "Don't be deceived." Don't fool yourself. Don't delude yourself. God will not be mocked. The word used in the Scriptures for *mocked* is a word that could be translated "ridiculed." God will not be laughed at. God will not be treated with contempt. Another way to translate this phrase is, "You cannot outwit God." The Bible is saying you are fooling yourself if you think you can fool God. He is omniscient and knows everything. Nothing escapes his knowledge. Luke 12:7 says: "The very hairs of your head are all numbered." In my case that's not much work, but for others it is a big job.

God sees everything. You cannot outwit God. Nor can you mock him—without consequences.

How do we mock God? When we claim to know him, yet continue in deliberate sin. There are a lot of people who think they are Christians. To them, being a Christian is merely acknowledging the existence of God—believing that God is out there somewhere. But even Satan believes in God, in the sense that he acknowledges his existence and power. James 2:19 tells us: "Even the demons believe—and tremble!"

So to merely believe in the existence of God is not enough.

Being a Christian means admitting we are sinners and turning from that sin, asking Jesus Christ to come into our hearts, then following him. Many people think that because they have taken part in some ritual or religious exercise such as baptism, Communion, or confession, their eternal destiny is sealed. But Jesus says, "Why do you call me 'Lord, Lord,' and not do the things that I say?" (see Matthew 7:21). The Bible says that if we love him, we will do what he tells us to do in his Word. We will keep his commandments.

We mock God when we say, "I love the Lord" but contradict and disobey his law. It's actually worse to go to church and pretend than it is to be a garden-variety unbeliever. A person who goes to church and pretends to be a follower of Jesus, yet deliberately and willfully lives apart from his standards, is in worse shape than the person out at the bar getting drunk on the weekend. At least the person in the bar may realize that he is a sinner and that he needs to get right with God one day. But the person sitting in the pew may be deceiving himself thinking, *Because I am doing this right now, I have satisfied God,* as though he were a pagan deity that could be appeased by some ritual or sacrifice on our part. We mock God when we live that way. We will reap what we sow.

Everything we have ever done will eventually catch up with us. We may think that we have covered our secrets. We may think our sin is well hidden and that no one will ever see it. But it will catch up; it always does. Someday we will have to stand in the courtroom of almighty God and be judged according to what we have done. The only hope is to give our lives to Christ. He then becomes our Mediator, our Representative, our Defense Attorney. That's the only way to avoid punishment on Judgment Day. If we keep on running from God, we will face the full consequences of our sin. We will reap the wages of sin not only in eternity but also right here on earth. The Bible says: "Because the sentence against an evil work is not executed speedily, therefore the heart of the sons of men is fully set in them to do evil" (Ecclesiastes 8:11).

Let me paraphrase: Because you don't get busted for your sin right away, you may think you can get away with it forever.

WHY DO I FEEL GUILTY?

Maybe you have done something wrong, but you haven't been caught. You have been fooling around, and nobody knows what you have done. You think, *I'm pulling it off.* Oh no, you aren't. It will eventually catch up with you—maybe today, maybe tomorrow, maybe a month from now. Sooner or later you will reap what you have sown. As God's inspired Word states: "Be sure your sin will find you out" (Numbers 32:23).

I read about a drug dealer who was turned in by an eighteen-month-old child. How can an eighteen-month-old turn in a drug dealer? Well, the drug-dealing dad was at home bagging cocaine and marijuana on the kitchen table, and the toddler crawled over to the telephone and by accident pushed the speed-dial number for 9-1-1. The police showed up and found Dad surrounded by drug paraphernalia and arrested him. His sin found him out.

> BECAUSE YOU DON'T GET BUSTED FOR YOUR SIN RIGHT AWAY, YOU MAY THINK YOU CAN GET AWAY WITH IT FOREVER.

I read an article in the newspaper about a hungry thief who stole some sausages from a meat market. When he grabbed a link and began to run with it, he hadn't bargained on the fact that many sausages were linked together. The links were forty-five feet long. He became entwined in the sausages. When the cops found him, he was trapped. His sin found him out.

Then there is the story about a thief who decided to steal some gasoline from a man's motor home in Seattle, Washington. He put a rubber siphoning hose into the tank and began to suck hard. Meanwhile, the man inside the motor home heard a noise outside that sounded like someone vomiting violently. He went outside and discovered that a fourteen-year-old youth had put his hose up to the septic tank instead of the gasoline tank. Poor kid. The man didn't press charges, thinking the boy had suffered enough. His sin had found him out.

Sin always finds us out—unless we come to Jesus Christ and ask him to forgive us of our sin. Even as Christians, sin may find us out from a human standpoint. But Jesus has removed the eternal consequences.

In the Old Testament book of Daniel, chapter 5, there is the story of King Belshazzar, who thought he could mock God. Belshazzar's grandfather Nebuchadnezzar had also been an unbelieving man for many years. But one day God got his attention and brought him to his senses. Apparently his grandson hadn't learned anything from Grandpa. One day this rebellious young king called in all of his princes and lords and ordered that the special cups and vessels used in the Jewish temple be brought in. He filled them with wine and toasted the gods of silver and gold. The Bible says that while he was drinking he saw something strange happening on the massive wall where military victories would normally be recorded. He saw a large disembodied hand writing some kind of mysterious message up there in the light of the candelabra he had ordered stolen from the temple. Later Belshazzar learned the interpretation of this heavenly graffiti from Daniel. It was a message from God that said, "You have been weighed in the balances, and found wanting" (v. 27).

When we stand on a scale, it usually shows that we weigh

more than we would like. But on God's scales we need to have some substance, some spiritual weight. This foolish and wicked king was a spiritual lightweight. On God's scales his life had no weight or substance. The message from God also said, "Your kingdom has been divided, and given to the Medes and Persians" (v. 28).

One moment King Belshazzar was on top of the world: powerful, feared by the citizens, doing whatever he pleased, and going out of his way to mock God. The next moment he had lost everything. His sin and mockery of God had caught up with him.

Daniel told Belshazzar that it was obvious he knew better but had sinned anyway. That's significant because knowledge always brings responsibility. Belshazzar's sin was greater because he knew what was right, ran from it, and deliberately defied God.

It's one thing to say, "I have never heard of Jesus Christ. I didn't know there was a God." But once we know there is a God who loves us enough to have sent his Son to die on a cross and pay for our sins, we must make a decision about Jesus. We can no longer passively stand back. Our eternal destiny depends on our response to Jesus.

□ □ □ □ □

This truth of reaping what we sow is a double-edged sword. It's true that if we sow to the flesh, we will reap corruption. But here is the good news: If we sow to the Spirit, we will reap life everlasting. If we walk with God and obey his Word, we will reap life and peace and joy.

It is true that I have given up a few things I used to enjoy doing now that I am a believer. My behavior is different than before I became a believer.

But what has the Christian really given up? While others have sown their wild oats, the Christian has sown spiritual seed. While others have pursued fun, the Christian has pursued faith. While others have pursued parties, the Christian has pursued prayer. While others have pursued sexual looseness, the Christian has pursued sexual purity. While others have pursued this earthly world, the Christian has pursued the heavenly one. While others have reaped corruption, the Christian has reaped life. While others feel used, the Christian feels new.

I look at some of my old friends and see the toll sin has taken on their lives. Some of them have been married two, three, or four times. I can see the physical toll that sin has taken on those who have tried to maintain the partying lifestyle. It eats away at them. It's such a rip-off. Satan takes advantage and keeps leading them down the path of waste and emptiness. Ultimately he wants them to face judgment in hell. Meanwhile God is saying to them, "Come to me. Walk in my plan for you."

Yes. I have given up a few things to follow Jesus Christ. But I think you will agree that none of these things were great sacrifices. I have given up sin. Misery. Loneliness. Emptiness. Ever-present guilt. Despair. Worries. Fear of death.

What has God given me in place of those things? Forgiveness. Fulfillment. Purpose. Hope of heaven. I have given up nothing compared to what God has given to me.

You might say, "Greg, I have done some horrible things."

Maybe so. But Jesus can put your past behind you. God can make you different on the inside. If you have sown to sin, you don't have to reap it. God can forgive you and put you on the road that leads to true life—one that is fulfilled, peaceful, and meaningful, as a Christian.

You might ask, "Well, what do I need to do? How do I make this step toward God? How do I receive forgiveness?

HOW DO I RECEIVE FORGIVENESS?

I once read about a man whose name had been mistakenly printed in the obituary column in his local newspaper. Can you imagine waking up in the morning and reading that you were no longer among the living? To be sure, it would be a little disconcerting. This man did what any of us would do in the same situation. He went down to the newspaper office and demanded to see the editor.

"This is terrible," he told the newspaper boss. "Because of your error, I am going to face embarrassment. And I will probably lose business. How could you do this to me?"

"Sir, I'm sorry," explained the editor. "It was a mistake. It was certainly not intentional."

But the man would not be consoled. He continued to rant and rave about the injustice of it all.

"Look, cheer up, buddy," the editor finally said. "Tomorrow I'll put your name in the birth column, and you can have a fresh start at life."

All of us have done things we regret. Wouldn't it be great if starting over were that easy?

Well, the Bible teaches that we *can* start over. We *can* have our slates wiped clean. Scripture tells us we can experience fundamental changes inside ourselves as well—changes that will help us avoid making the mistakes of the past again in the future. How do we accomplish these things?

Jesus gave us this hope when he said, "You must be born again" (John 3:7). He described a new birth, a new life. Second Corinthians 5:17 says: "If anyone is in Christ, he is a new creation; old things have passed away; behold, all things have become new." Yes, it is possible to be changed.

For instance, just look at the New Testament example of the life of a man known as Saul of Tarsus. He experienced one of the most unexpected and radical conversions in the history of the Christian church. It was so unexpected that initially his conversion was greeted by skepticism and suspicion. This man Saul had once dedicated his life to the destruction of the Christian church. He was a man hell-bent on destroying everything about Christianity. He persecuted men and women who chose to follow Jesus as their Messiah. But once he had his own encounter with Jesus on the road to Damascus, he was radically changed—forever. This zealot who had formerly been controlled by hate was controlled by love from then on. A name that would once send chills down the spine of a Christian, Saul of Tarsus was transformed into one of the greatest preachers in the history of the Christian church. He was even given a new name—Paul the apostle.

Paul's conversion was such an unlikely event that a British agnostic of the last century thought it would not be difficult to disprove it. He set out to prove that the New Testament lacked credibility. The agnostic was determined to undermine the foundation of the Christian faith by getting to the "truth" about Paul. George Littleton was a true scholar. His book was called *Observations on the Conversion and Apostleship of Saint Paul.* But his conclusion was remarkably different from his original thesis. What did he discover? "Paul's conversion and apostleship alone, duly considered, are a demonstration sufficient to prove Christianity to be a divine revelation."

A funny thing happened to Littleton in the midst of his investigation. He ended up meeting the same Jesus who had changed Saul of Tarsus so dramatically on the road to Damascus. He became a believer after studying Saul's conversion. Previously Littleton had thought it was not possible for a man so opposed to the church to become a believer. But he found out that it is possible.

The story of how Saul of Tarsus became Paul the apostle shows that no one is beyond redemption. It's a lesson for all of us. It shows that it doesn't matter how radical we once were; it doesn't matter how hard-hearted we may currently be. It doesn't matter what lifestyle we may be trapped in. There is hope for each and all of us.

Who was Saul of Tarsus? He was a young man who never did anything halfheartedly. Saul was raised in a strict Jewish home. He learned the Scripture as a young boy. His family tree sprouted from the best soil. He was of the tribe of Benjamin— the tribe of Israel's first king, Saul. Possibly Saul of Tarsus was even named after him.

Saul decided early in his life to go into the ministry. He

became a Pharisee, which meant that he was a highly dedicated religious individual, a disciplined student of the Scriptures and other writings of this strict religious sect. Because of their intense jealousy, the Pharisees were the prime movers behind the crucifixion of Jesus.

It just goes to show how religion can be a blinding and destructive force. Many horrible crimes and sins have been committed in the name of religion throughout history—sadly, some even in the name of Christianity. I know people who will not listen to a gospel message because of abuses done to them in the name of the Cross or Jesus.

So here was Saul, a religious man, convinced he was doing the right thing. But he was actually fighting God. Saul did not persecute the church because he was a bad man. He did it because he thought he was following truth—just doing what was right. He honestly believed that these strange people known as Christians were a menace to God. But following his conversion he wrote: "I did it ignorantly in unbelief" (1 Timothy 1:13).

Later Saul became a member of the supreme court of that day—the Jewish Sanhedrin—where he enjoyed fame and influence. He had risen to the top of his profession. This is where we are introduced to him in Acts 8:1-3:

> Now Saul was consenting to [Stephen's] death. At that time a great persecution arose against the church which was at Jerusalem; and they were scattered throughout the regions of Judea and Samaria, except the apostles. And devout men carried Stephen to his burial, and made great lamentation over him. As for Saul, he made havoc of the church, entering

every house, and dragging off men and women, committing them to prison.

What motivated Saul? Why was he filled with so much hatred and venom? Acts 7:54-60 records the reasons. It is a dramatic account of the death of the first martyr of the Christian church, a courageous young man named Stephen. Stephen stood before the Sanhedrin and boldly proclaimed the gospel.

When they heard these things they were cut to the heart, and they gnashed at him with their teeth. But he, being full of the Holy Spirit, gazed into heaven and saw the glory of God, and Jesus standing at the right hand of God, and said, "Look! I see the heavens opened and the Son of Man standing at the right hand of God!" Then they cried out with a loud voice, stopped their ears, and ran at him with one accord; and they cast him out of the city and stoned him. And the witnesses laid down their clothes at the feet of a young man named Saul. And they stoned Stephen as he was calling on God and saying, "Lord Jesus, receive my spirit." Then he knelt down and cried out with a loud voice, "Lord, do not charge them with this sin." And when he had said this, he fell asleep.

> MANY HORRIBLE CRIMES AND SINS HAVE BEEN COMMITTED IN THE NAME OF RELIGION THROUGHOUT HISTORY.

147

What a powerful testimony this was to Saul. Even in the face of death, Stephen was praying for mercy on the ones who had been responsible for his death. It reminds us of Jesus hanging on the cross. "Father, forgive them, for they do not know what they do" (Luke 23:34). That statement radically transformed the attitude and outlook of one of the thieves crucified beside Jesus who turned to him in a moment and with a flash of belief says, " 'Lord, remember me when You come into Your kingdom.' And Jesus said to him, 'Assuredly, I say to you, today you will be with Me in Paradise' " (Luke 23:42-43).

As Stephen made a similar plea to the Lord, it apparently penetrated the hardened heart of Saul of Tarsus. Who knows what was going through Stephen's mind at that very moment? He probably thought, *Wow, what an opportunity! The Jewish Sanhedrin. Imagine what would happen if one of these people came to the faith. What could one of these men do for the kingdom of God? I am going to proclaim the gospel. Maybe one of them will believe.*

Initially, Stephen's plea caused Saul's heart to grow harder. He began to persecute believers even more zealously, perhaps because he was convicted by the Holy Spirit.

What does it mean to be convicted by the Holy Spirit?

It is when God brings an awareness of your own sinfulness and need for forgiveness. It is when you find yourself more empty than ever, when the pleasures and treasures of the world no longer satisfy you. It is a sense of your need for God.

I have often noticed that those who argue the most may be the closest to believing in Jesus Christ—closer, in fact, than those who are passive and even somewhat agreeable.

For instance, there may be people in your office or place of work who know you are a Christian. Some will say, "I'm glad *you've* found God. You seem to be much happier. I'm happy for *you.*" They don't necessarily argue with you. They don't make fun of you. They have even agreed to go to church with you sometime in the distant future. You conclude that person is really close to coming to Jesus Christ. They're so open!

Then there is that one belligerent person who has given you a hard time ever since he found out you were a Christian. He argues with you constantly. Every day he challenges you with a new question just to irritate you. You conclude he is really against God. I've found that this is often the opposite of what seems obvious.

There is an old proverb that says, "When you throw a stone into a pack of dogs, the one that barks the loudest is the one that got hit!"

Those who are always challenging and arguing with you may be closer than you think to the kingdom of God. They may be under the conviction of the Holy Spirit, protesting the most, or "barking" the loudest, because they got hit!

This was clearly the case with Saul. Still stinging from the incredible witness of young Stephen, he went out of his way to hunt down Christians.

Saul used the occasion of Stephen's trial and execution to launch a full-scale persecution of the new church. He carried off converts, both men and women, to prison. He even obtained extradition papers from the high priest and set off for Damascus, 140 miles from Jerusalem, to arrest more Christians. Some believers had escaped his net and fled to Damascus, where several synagogues served a large Jewish colony. So Saul planned to hunt them down and drag them back. No one was going to get away with worshiping Jesus as long as Saul was around!

But an unexpected thing happened on his journey:

Then Saul, still breathing threats and murder against the disciples of the Lord, went to the high priest and asked for letters from him to the synagogues of Damascus, so that if he found any who were of the Way, whether men or women, he might bring them bound to Jerusalem. And as he journeyed he came near Damascus, and suddenly a light shone around him from heaven. Then he fell to the ground, and heard a voice saying to him, "Saul, Saul, why are you persecuting Me?" And he said, "Who are You, Lord?" Then the Lord said, "I am Jesus, whom you are persecuting. It is hard for you to kick against the goads." So he, trembling and astonished, said, "Lord, what do You want me to do?" Then the Lord said to him, "Arise and go into the city, and you will be told what you must do." And the men who journeyed with him stood speechless, hearing a voice but seeing no one. . . . But they led him by the hand and brought him into Damascus. And he was three days without sight, and neither ate nor drank. (Acts 9:1-9)

Up to this point Saul was living on hatred. When it says he was "breathing threats," that means threats were sustaining him. Another translation of the original text states that he was like a wild beast seeking out his prey. He smelled the blood of Christians. His heart was so filled with hatred and his mind so poisoned with prejudice that he later said that a raging fury had obsessed him. At that point, however, the resurrected Jesus got ahold of him and the Lord said, "Why are you persecuting Me?"

Imagine how Saul felt at that moment. He asked, "Who are you, Lord?" He was probably thinking to himself: *Don't let him say Jesus. Oh, please don't let him say Jesus!* And, of course, the Lord replied, "I am Jesus." Saul must have thought: *Oh no. I knew he was going to say that. I've been sinning against the very one I thought I was serving!* Imagine how those words must have reverberated through Saul's soul at that moment. He awoke one day to realize that instead of serving

> AN OLD PROVERB: "WHEN YOU THROW A STONE INTO A PACK OF DOGS, THE ONE THAT BARKS THE LOUDEST IS THE ONE THAT GOT HIT!"

God, he had actually been opposing God. Now he was colliding with him. What a shock!

□ □ □ □ □

I remember the first day that I had been against Jesus. All my life I thought I was a Christian because whenever I was in trouble, I prayed to God. When a crisis hit, it was straight to Jesus for me. It was always Jesus I called on because I knew he was out there somewhere. So I thought, *I'm a Christian. Of course I am. I call on Jesus when I'm in trouble. I must be a Christian.*

One day I attended a meeting of true Christians on the front lawn of my high school, as I mentioned in the introduction of this book. As the teens were worshiping the Lord and singing, I looked around and thought, *These people have lost their minds. Why do they do this?* I used to make fun of these kids. I laughed at them. They were a joke to me to watch them on campus carrying their Bibles around, wearing smiles on their faces. I thought, *What a bunch of fools! Why don't they keep their religion to themselves?* I was hardly a person who was interested in their lifestyle. But one day, out of sheer curiosity as to why they would behave the way they did, I attended one of their meetings. I sat close enough to hear what they were saying, but not close enough so my friends would think I had joined their ranks. (That would have meant social suicide in high school in those days.) It was then that I realized that I had thought I was a Christian but was really against Jesus. A man spoke that day who quoted Jesus as saying, "You are for me or against me." I looked around at those Christians, kids we called "Jesus freaks" back in the sixties, and I thought, *They are definitely for him. No question. They really seem to know him in some kind of personal way.* I looked at myself and reasoned, *I'm not one of them. I don't know him that way. I didn't even realize until now that I could! That means I'm against him.* I certainly didn't want to be against Jesus. I wanted to be *for* him. I realized that day that I had been against God when I thought I was for him. That's what Saul realized.

Saul had been made ready for this moment. His heart had been softening, even while he was condemning believers to death and torture. It's interesting how Jesus used the expression "It is hard for you to kick against the goads." A goad was a sharpened stick, a primitive instrument used to jab into the body or legs of the animal pulling a plow, wagon, or chariot. It was designed to get the animal to go faster. If the animal wasn't moving fast enough, the farmer just took out the goad and poked the animal. In other words, Jesus was telling Saul, "I have been trying to penetrate your hardened heart. You are fighting me and resisting what I am trying to do."

One of those goads may well have been the witness of Stephen. When Saul watched that brave young man praying for the very people who were condemning him to death, I have to believe Saul's heart was moved, though he probably didn't show it outwardly. I can just imagine he had his arms crossed, a scowl on his face. But inside he must have been thinking, *Where does he get the courage to face death so peacefully? And why is he praying for mercy for us?*

Certainly the spread of the gospel and the response of the believers were like goads. The more Saul tried to stop the gospel, the faster it spread. He couldn't stop this impassioned church from proliferating, no matter how hard he tried. Each one of these goads helped to ultimately bring Saul to his senses and to the living God he had been so zealously fighting against.

Often I am asked what it means to be a Christian. We can learn much by observing the way Saul quickly changed after his dramatic conversion. Immediately after his conversion we find Saul praying—one of the attributes and characteristics of a true Christian. He may have been praying for the forgiveness of his sins. He had much to be sorry for—considering all those he had persecuted. He was responsible for the death of Stephen. But now he was a new man with a new heart.

Later we see him preaching. The former persecutor of Christians was now working to convert others to Christianity. With a changed heart full of thanksgiving, he proceeded to turn the world upside down for Jesus Christ. We are sometimes surprised when we hear of notorious sinners becoming committed Christians. This should not surprise us at all. For Jesus said that those who have been forgiven much love much more.

When he was on the Damascus road, Saul asked God two questions that each of us should ask. The first was, "Who are you?" The answer to that question will take a lifetime to discover. We need to know who the Lord is. Even when we find out he is Jesus, we have more to learn.

I will happily spend the rest of my life discovering who Jesus is. I can't think of a better thing in which to invest my life. Paul later wrote what his goal in life was in Philippians 3:10: "That I may know Him."

The second question Saul asked God was, "What will you have me do?" Many Christians live unproductive lives because they fail to ask this question. If they are honest, they would say something like, "Lord, what will you do for *me?* How are you going to make my life better? How are you going to make my life fuller?"

The better questions are: "What will you have me do? What are your plans for me, Lord? What is your purpose for me?"

Sometimes it is necessary for us to ask God certain key questions, as Saul did, in order to receive the answers we need. In other instances, seeking the answers requires a lifetime of pursuit, study, and prayer. But the answers are there. They are found in a relationship with God through Jesus Christ. All of the answers are there—although some questions will not be answered this side of eternity. One day, when as Christians we see Jesus face-to-face, every one of our questions will be answered and resolved.

☐ ☐ ☐ ☐ ☐

Books about spiritual issues are the hottest things going today. Our quest for answers makes them the best-selling topic of the day. Yet all of this interest in spiritual matters is nothing new. We have been made in the image of God. God created each of us with a void inside—an emptiness—that only he can fill. It is as if we were made with a God-shaped hole in our hearts. Attempting to fill it with anything but him is futile. Augustine said, "You have made us for yourself, and our souls are restless until they find their rest in you."

Jesus met a woman drawing water at a well. This woman had a void in her life that she had apparently tried to fill with relationships with men. She had gone to that well, so to speak, many times—five times, to be exact, for that is how many times she had been married and divorced. She was living with a man to whom she was not married at the time she met Jesus. A Samaritan, she was a woman who had lived a hard life. Used and abused by men, she had no doubt received the short end of the stick.

When she met Jesus at the well, she was surprised that he, being a Jew, would even talk to her because the Jews and

Samaritans had a long-standing feud and prejudices passed from generation to generation. Even so, Jesus asked her for a drink and said to her, "Whoever drinks of this water will thirst again" (John 4:13). She had no idea what he was talking about and thought he was talking literally about the well water. But he was talking about the deepest thirst of life—the thirst within her soul.

We could write the same message over other "wells." It ought to be emblazoned over the well of success. The well of possessions should be clearly marked with this cautionary statement. There should be a notice like this at the well of pleasure. In each instance Jesus says, "If you drink of this, you will thirst again. You will never get enough. You will always come up wanting more." Proverbs 27:20 says: "Hell and Destruction are never full; so the eyes of man are never satisfied."

When we realize that God made us and wants us to come into a relationship with him, we will then find the meaning of life. We won't find it by seeking happiness or by trying to find fulfillment in worldly successes, possessions, and pleasures. We can find real meaning in life only by coming to know God and his plan and purpose for us. The wonderful result is that we will become happy and fulfilled people. Psalm 144:15 says: "Happy are the people whose God is the Lord!"

Jesus said, "But seek first the kingdom of God and His righteousness, and all these things shall be added to you" (Matthew 6:33). In other words, a new set of priorities will put God in the forefront of your life. Seek to live a life that is pleasing to God. Then you will find everything you are looking for. You will find fulfillment. You will find joy. You will find peace.

In the biblical account of the Prodigal Son, Jesus tells the dramatic story of a young man who had decided to leave his father's house (see Luke 15:11-32). He probably felt his father had been holding him back from "the good life." So one day he blatantly demanded his portion of the family inheritance, and with money in his pocket and a spring in his step, he left home and commenced to live as he pleased. He went far away to a foreign country, where happiness and fulfillment seemed to be defined by eating and drinking and nice clothes and sex. The son spent his fortune in pursuit of pleasure. Things haven't really changed all that much since then, have they? People are still obsessed with those things today. But after the Prodigal Son had been out of his father's house for a while, he came up empty. He ended up broke. He was left all alone. So he returned home. And the Prodigal found that everything he was searching for in life was right there in his father's house; it had been there all along. What did he go out looking for? One thing was clothes. When he came home, his father said, "Put a beautiful robe on him." Another thing he was searching for was pleasure and fun. His father said, "Let's have a party." Another desire of his heart was for food. His father said, "Let's have a great feast together." He found everything he wanted in his father's house.

In the same way, we can find everything we need in life in a relationship with God through Jesus Christ.

☐   ☐   ☐   ☐   ☐

One cold December day I was on my way to New York City, connecting through Chicago as I usually do when flying across the country from my home in southern California. As I walked through the terminal, a large advertisement caught my eye. It was a tropical beach scene with beautiful turquoise blue water, white sand, the shining sun, and an empty beach chair.

Nothing could have been more appealing to me at that moment. It was most alluring, given my circumstances, wandering around in a Chicago airport terminal during freezing weather. Something in that photograph represented what all of us want—rest and relaxation. We all want to relax. We all want to feel safe. We want to feel protected. We want to feel secure. We want to feel rested.

In 1930 an unusual event took place. It still represents an open case in the FBI missing-persons files. On August 15, after dining out with his family, a New York State Supreme Court justice named Joseph Crater hailed a taxi and was never seen or heard from again. The FBI thought the disappearance might be work related as the judge had heard many mob cases. But there was no real evidence to support that theory. All investigations led to dead ends. The only clue was a note he left for his wife and family. It said, "I am very, very tired. Love, Joe." That was it. That was the last anyone ever heard from him.

I think many of us feel that way today. Jesus has something to say to the person who is exhausted, to the person who is worn out, chewed up, and spit out by life. He offers rest to those who are frustrated, hurting, and tired.

In Matthew 11:28-30 Jesus made this statement: "Come to Me, all you who labor and are heavy laden, and I will give you rest. Take My yoke upon you and learn from Me, for I am gentle and lowly in heart, and you will find rest for your souls. For My yoke is easy and My burden is light."

An expanded translation of this same verse goes like this:

"Come here to me all you who are growing weary to the point of exhaustion and who have been loaded with burdens and are bending beneath their weight. I alone will cause you to cease from your labor and take away your burdens and refresh you with rest."

This is the Christian life in a nutshell. This is what it is like to walk with Jesus Christ.

□ □ □ □ □

Is it possible to change? Is there really a fresh start available to us through Jesus? How can this wonderful promise be ours? Can we really experience this rest that Jesus is describing? Is it really addressed to all of us? Do we qualify?

Jesus did not say, "Come unto me all of you who are rich." Nor did he say, "Come unto me all of you who are perfect." He didn't say, "Come unto me all of you who are successful," or "Come unto me all of you who are beautiful or handsome." His promise wasn't addressed to perfect or flawless people. It was addressed to people who are weary—people who have been beaten down by life. It was addressed to those who have seen the enormity of their sin and are being crushed beneath the weight of the cares of life. Sin promises life but ultimately brings death. It promises happiness but brings emptiness. It promises pleasure but brings pain and guilt. Jesus extended this invitation to people who are worn out from their futile search for truth through human wisdom—and to those who have labored through countless efforts of religious rituals and are still empty.

From John 3:1-21 we see the example of the great religious leader Nicodemus. He was a respected man, revered for his spirituality. But Nicodemus came to Jesus by night looking for answers. In spite of his fame, in spite of his position, in spite of his religion, he was still empty, searching, and laden down with the burdens of life.

We also have the example of the rich young ruler. He had everything, including position and authority. He had kept the commandments since he was a young boy. But in spite of his good morality, power, and prestige, he still came to Jesus asking the question "Good Teacher, what shall I do that I may inherit eternal life?" (Mark 10:17).

Here is Jesus' answer: "Sell whatever you have and give to the poor . . . and follow Me" (v. 21). That's it . . . so simple . . . yet so profound. Just come. "Follow Me."

The same invitation is echoed throughout Scripture. In Isaiah 1:18, God states, " 'Come now, and let us reason together,' says the Lord, 'though your sins are like scarlet, they shall be as white as snow; though they are red like crimson, they shall be as wool.' "

Revelation 22:17 says: "The Spirit and the bride say, 'Come!' And let him who hears say, 'Come!' And let him who thirsts come. Whoever desires, let him take the water of life freely."

Isaiah 55:1-3 says: "Everyone who thirsts, come to the waters; and you who have no money, come, buy and eat. Yes, come, buy wine and milk without money and without price. Why do you spend money for what is not bread, and your wages for what does not satisfy? Listen carefully to Me, and eat what is good, and let your soul delight itself in abundance. Incline your ear, and come to Me. Hear, and your soul shall live."

That's what Jesus always says: "Just come to me." Notice he doesn't say, "Learn of me first." Nor does he say, "Take my yoke upon you first," or "First make some changes in your life." At the initial point, all he says is, "Come. Come as you are. Come with your problems. Come with your guilt. Come with your sin. Come. Don't let anything hold you back."

Our modern culture would give us a different answer. It would say, "If you can just get that promotion . . . if you can just get that car . . . if you can just get that house . . . if you can just have that vacation . . . then you will find the rest you are seeking."

Materialism would say, "Build it up, and you will find rest."

Pleasure mania would say, "Live it up, and you will find rest."

Religion would say, "Keep it up, and you will find rest."

Jesus says, "Come to me, and you will find rest. Just come to me."

☐ ☐ ☐ ☐ ☐

Do you yearn for that kind of rest? Do you want a fresh start? Do you want your life to be transformed like Saul's? You can experience these things right now. And you won't need to have your obituary printed prematurely in the newspaper in order to have it. All you need to do is come to Jesus.

But how is that done?

First of all, you must recognize that you are a sinner. Realize that you have missed the mark. This is true of each of us. We have deliberately crossed the line not once but many times. The Bible says: "All have sinned and fall short of the glory of God" ((Romans 3:23). This is a hard admission for many to make, but if we are not willing to hear the bad news, we cannot appreciate and respond to the *Good News*.

Second, we must realize that Jesus Christ died on the cross for us. Because of sin, God had to take drastic measures to reach us. So he came to this earth and walked here as a man. But Jesus was more than just a good man. He was the God-man—God incarnate—and that is why his death on the cross is so significant.

At the cross, God himself—in the person of Jesus Christ—took our place and bore our sins. He paid for them and purchased our redemption.

Third, we must repent of our sin. God has commanded men everywhere to repent. Acts 3:19 states: "Repent therefore and be converted, that your sins may be blotted out, so that times of refreshing may come from the presence of the Lord." What does this word *repent* mean? It means to change direction—to hang a U-turn on the road of life. It means to stop living the kind of life we led previously and start living the kind of life outlined in the pages of the Bible. Now we must change and be willing to make a break with the past.

Fourth, we must receive Jesus Christ into our hearts and lives. Being a Christian is having God himself take residence in our lives. John 1:12 tells us, "But as many as received Him, to them He gave the right to become children of God." We must receive him. Jesus said, "Behold, I stand at the door and knock. If anyone hears My voice and opens the door, I will come in" (Revelation 3:20). Each one of us must individually decide to open the door. How do we open it? Through prayer.

If you have never asked Jesus Christ to come into your life, you can do it right now. Here is a prayer you might pray:

Lord Jesus, I know that I am a sinner, and I am sorry for my sin. I turn and repent of my sins right now. Thank you for dying on the cross for me and paying the price for my sin. Please come into my heart and life right now. Fill me with your Holy Spirit, and help me to be your disciple. Thank you for forgiving me and coming into my life. Thank you that I am now a child of yours and that I am going to heaven. In Jesus' name, I pray. Amen.

When you pray that prayer, God will respond to you. You have made the right decision—the decision that will impact how you spend eternity. Now you will go to heaven, and in the meantime find peace and the answers to your spiritual questions. Congratulations! You just made a big decision—the most important decision anyone can make. One you will never regret.

WHAT NOW?

CHAPTER 9

In 1948 a man named Jim Elliot wrote these words in his journal: "I seek not a long life but a full one like you, Lord Jesus." Jim Elliot was martyred by the Auca Indians for his faith in Jesus Christ and his efforts to carry the gospel to them as a missionary. That's commitment! Elliot's dramatic story is chronicled in the powerful book Through Gates of Splendor, *written by his wife, Elisabeth.*

The quality of one's life cannot be measured in terms of years. Some who have lived a long time have not lived full lives. The bottom line is this: An abundant life on earth is connected to our eternal life in heaven. Or, as C. S. Lewis put it: "Aim for heaven, and you will get earth thrown in. Aim at earth, and you get neither."

When you aim at heaven and recognize that your life will reach far beyond this relatively brief span of time we spend on earth, you will receive eternal life with earth thrown in. You will receive a full, rich life with purpose and direction if you choose to walk with Jesus Christ. But if you aim only at earth and at the things this temporal life brings, you'll receive neither earth nor heaven.

▫ ▫ ▫ ▫ ▫

Remember the rebellious and drunken King Belshazzar who saw a finger writing words on the wall—*Mene, Mene, Tekel, Upharsin* (see Daniel 5:24-28)? "They have brought the vessels of His house before you, and you and your lords, your wives and your concubines, have drunk wine from them. And you have praised the gods of silver and gold, bronze and iron, wood and stone, which do not see or hear or know; and the God who holds your breath in His hand and owns all your ways, you have not glorified" (v. 23).

The essential mistake Belshazzar made was that he had failed to glorify and honor God. The same is true of many of us today. We fail to fulfill the purposes for which God created us—to know him and to glorify him.

Jesus said in John 15:1-8:

I am the true vine, and My Father is the vinedresser. Every branch in Me that does not bear fruit He takes away; and every branch that bears fruit He prunes, that it may bear more fruit. You are already clean because of the word which I have spoken to you. Abide in Me, and I in you. As the branch cannot bear fruit of itself, unless it abides in the vine, neither can you, unless you abide in Me. I am the vine, you are the branches. He who abides in Me, and I in him, bears much fruit; for without Me you can do nothing. If anyone does not abide in Me, he is cast out as a branch and is withered; and they gather them and throw them into the fire, and they are burned. If you abide in Me, and My words abide in you, you will ask what you desire, and it shall be done for you. By this My Father is glorified, that you bear much fruit; so you will be My disciples.

How do we glorify God? By bearing fruit, Jesus said. That is the answer. We were placed on this earth primarily to enter into a relationship with our Creator and to bear fruit for him.

What does it mean to bear fruit? The concept of bearing fruit in Scripture is often used to describe the results of someone having a relationship with Jesus Christ. In Mark 4:20 Jesus said, "These are the ones sown on good ground, those who hear the word, accept it, and bear fruit." Jesus also said in Matthew 7:20, "By their fruits you will know them." Colossians 1:10 says: "Walk worthy of the Lord, fully pleasing Him, being fruitful in every good work and increasing in the knowledge of God." There it is. *Love God. Know God.* Then, as an outgrowth of that, *you will bear fruit.*

Everything in this temporal life is secondary—your career, what you do with your free time, what you do in other areas. All of that must take a backseat to knowing God and bearing fruit.

Christians can easily become distracted with other aspects of their lives that cause them to lose sight of their primary objectives—to love God, to know him, to glorify him, and to bear fruit.

What happens if we don't bear fruit? John 15:5 says: "He who abides in Me, and I in him, bears much fruit."

To understand this vine that Jesus is describing in John 15, think of a grapevine, not a fruit tree. A vine is of little use other than to bear fruit. You can't build a house from vines. Even when vines are cast into the fire, they flame up and quickly burn out. So vines won't even keep you warm. Jesus said: "I am the true vine, and My Father is the vinedresser" (John 15:1).

God intended Israel to bear fruit and to glorify his name before the nations of the world. But he said through the prophet Hosea, "Israel empties his vine; he brings forth fruit for himself" (Hosea 10:1).

That's true of so many of us. We live only for ourselves, thinking about what we want in life or of what we can get out of it. Then when we come to Jesus Christ, we want to know what he can do for us.

That is why I don't like it when the gospel message is presented as some sort of "success package." Jesus Christ does not promise to make you rich, thin, or to grow hair on your head. He does, however, promise to enrich your life, to give it meaning and purpose, and the wonderful hope of life beyond the grave in a place called heaven.

As I have already stated, there has to come a point in our Christian lives when we start asking, "Lord, what do you want me to do for you?" instead of, "What can you do for me? How can you help me? How can you bless me?"

"Lord," Paul asked on the Damascus road, "what do You want me to do?" (Acts 9:6). The secret to living the Christian life to its fullest is bearing fruit. God did not create you, and Jesus Christ did not die for you just so you might go through life merely receiving. God created you, and Jesus Christ purchased you so that you might know him and invest your life in giving.

□ □ □ □ □

What is this fruit that Jesus is seeking? Many times the phrase "bearing fruit" is used in the New Testament.

Paul wrote to his friends in Romans 1:13: "I often planned to come to you . . . that I might have some fruit among you also, just as among the other Gentiles." He was talking about fruit in the context of leading others to faith. Proverbs 11:30 says: "The fruit of the righteous is a tree of life, and he who wins souls is wise." Jesus said, "By this My Father is glorified, that you bear much fruit" (John 15:8). How can we do that? One way to bear fruit is by winning others to Jesus Christ and helping them to grow spiritually.

> JESUS CHRIST DOES NOT PROMISE TO MAKE YOU RICH, THIN, OR TO GROW HAIR ON YOUR HEAD. HE DOES, HOWEVER, PROMISE TO ENRICH YOUR LIFE, TO GIVE IT MEANING AMD PURPOSE, AND THE WONDERFUL HOPE OF LIFE BEYOND THE GRAVE IN A PLACE CALLED HEAVEN.

To some, God gives that privilege often; to others, not so often. Regardless of what part you play in the process, God wants you to be prepared for your role as a soul winner. He may call you to sow seeds. You may find yourself watering the seeds that others have sown. You may have the privilege of reaping the seeds that others have sown and watered. But in one way, shape, or form, God wants you to be a part of the chain that brings people to faith in Christ. You have a part to play. You are a vital link in that chain through the faithful witness of your Christian life.

Let me illustrate how this process works with a story about a man who played a significant role in modern church history. He was not a pastor or an author. He wasn't a missionary. He was a man who sought to bear fruit for God by sharing the gospel.

His name was Edward Kimble. Most of us don't know that name. Edward Kimble was a Sunday school teacher in his church. He sensed God's leading to share the gospel with a shoe salesman, but he couldn't muster up the courage. So he paced around the store several times until he finally had an idea of what he wanted to say. Then he went into the back storeroom, found this young man named Dwight, and shared the gospel with him. Young Dwight became a Christian and went on to have a preaching ministry. He was known as D. L. Moody—the greatest evangelist in church history, up to that point.

Several years later, when Moody was preaching, a pastor named Frederick B. Meyer was listening and was deeply stirred. As a result he went into a nationwide preaching ministry. A young college student named Wilbur Chapman accepted Christ while listening to one of F. B. Meyer's sermons. When Chapman went into an evangelistic crusade ministry, he hired a young professional baseball player named Billy Sunday. Then the call of God came upon Billy Sunday to preach the gospel. He became the renowned evangelist of his time, preaching to countless thousands. One time Mr. Sunday held an evangelistic crusade in Charlotte, North Carolina. A group of businessmen were so moved by what God had done, they decided to sponsor another crusade. Sunday couldn't come so they brought in another preacher named Mordecai Ham. Ham's meetings were not that well attended. They pitched an old tent outside town, laid the sawdust down on the ground, but not many people came forward to receive Christ at those meetings. Yet on the final night a tall, lanky farm boy made his way up the aisle. He was known to his friends as Billy Frank. Today we know him as Billy Graham.

It all started with Edward Kimble who mustered up the courage to share the gospel with D. L. Moody . . . who touched F. B. Meyer . . . who touched Wilbur Chapman . . . who touched Billy Sunday . . . who indirectly touched Mordecai Ham . . . who touched Billy Graham.

By this story we can see that we will never know how many souls will be affected when we lead just one person to Christ.

Another kind of fruit is our change in conduct and character. Galatians 5:22 says: "The fruit of the Spirit is love, joy, peace, longsuffering, kindness, goodness, faithfulness, gentleness, self-control." These are traits that should be found in the lives of the followers of Jesus Christ. Remember, Jesus said, "By their fruits you will know them" (Matthew 7:20). There should be fruit in our lives—meaning there should be a change taking place in our hearts, in our attitudes, in our actions.

Sometimes I think we Christians ought to hang signs around our necks that say Under Construction. We all have a long way to go. There are times when I think I am really becoming Christlike. And then something will happen that reminds me how far short of the mark I still fall. Being conformed into the image of Jesus Christ is a lifelong process.

□ □ □ □ □

Take a look at your own life. Are you bearing spiritual fruit? Are love and joy, peace and gentleness, faith and self-control in your life? Or do you have hatred and bitterness, gloom and turmoil, harshness and worry and arrogance?

If you are already a believer, decide whether you need to recommit your life to Christ. Ask God for the fruit of the Spirit to be manifested in your life so you will become more like Jesus.

The only way to produce this fruit is found in John 15:4, where Jesus says, "Abide in Me, and I in you. As the branch cannot bear fruit of itself, unless it abides in the vine, neither can you, unless you abide in Me." Here is the secret of spiritual growth. What does it mean to abide? Think of the word *abide* as having permanence of position—a continuing commitment.

> WE WILL NEVER KNOW HOW MANY SOULS WILL BE AFFECTED WHEN WE LEAD JUST ONE PERSON TO CHRIST.

Consider what would happen if you were to take a beautiful tree that was planted in your front yard and uproot it. Maybe you just decided one day, "This tree is blocking my view. I want it in my backyard." So, you dig it up, roots and all, and go to the backyard to dig a huge hole. You put the tree in, put the soil back on top again, and then the tree begins to take root in the backyard and grow once more.

Then you say, "I liked it better in the front yard." So you rip it up again, take it back into the front yard, and plant it again. Then just as it is starting to take root again you decide, "The backyard—that's the place." And you uproot it again. That tree is going to go into shock. It's going to die. You can't keep uprooting a tree and planting it again and again if you expect it to survive and grow.

In the same way there are people who say, "I'm going to follow Jesus Christ. I'm going to live the Christian life. This is the year when I am going to walk with the Lord. I am going to church. I am going to pray." But after a month goes by, they say, "I don't know. I have other things I want to do. I don't think I really have time for all this." So they uproot themselves and go back to the old lifestyle. Then they quickly realize how empty that is and go back to church again. They go back into the spiritual pursuits. Then they are drawn back into the old life again. Individuals who do this are like that tree: ripped up and planted, ripped up again and replanted. They will not bring forth spiritual fruit doing that; they must sink their roots deep down in Jesus Christ—and stay put. It's a continuing commitment.

Jesus said, "If anyone desires to come after Me, let him deny himself, and take up his cross *daily*, and follow Me" (Luke 9:23, emphasis mine). That means maintaining unbroken fellowship with God.

▫ ▫ ▫ ▫ ▫

Living in America, we are always on the go, always moving here and there. It's hard for us to just slow down. But this is what must be done if we are to grow spiritually. We must abide in Jesus Christ.

"He who says he abides in Him ought himself also to walk just as He walked," states 1 John 2:6. *Walking* is a steady motion.

King David prayed in Psalm 51:10, "Create in me a clean heart . . . and renew a steadfast spirit within me." We must have that consistency in our lives spiritually to stay rooted in Jesus Christ.

What does this mean, practically speaking? Someone might say, "That's great in theory. But how do I do this? How do I abide? What things must I do on a daily basis?"

It means that you set priorities. Recognize that God must be at the top of the list. You don't work him in after you have done everything else. You work everything else in after you have taken time for him. That means that each day you will need to take time for God and his Word. It means you will need to take time in prayer.

Also, to abide means to be with God's people. The Bible tells us not to forsake the assembling of ourselves together, as the manner of some is (Hebrews 10:25). Have you ever noticed how people find excuses not to go to church? "Things came up," they'll say. I am always amazed to find that a little rain will keep some people away from church. But it won't keep them away from the mall—or the movie theater. It all comes down to priorities.

□ □ □ □ □

When I started pastoring many years ago, I was convinced that God had called me to be an evangelist. I was certain that my calling was to travel around and preach the gospel. But a small Bible study began to develop, and young people were attending. I was young myself—nineteen years old when I first started pastoring. I realized I was not qualified for such a task. I had been a Christian for only two years. My Bible knowledge was somewhat limited. But this group of young people began to grow and ultimately became the core group of the church I pastor today. I looked for other people to take over this ministry because I was convinced I was called to be an evangelist. But God had different plans for me. He called me to be a pastor. I didn't like it at first. I didn't want to do that. I dug my heels in and tried to find a way out. But as time passed I began to love pastoring. I still love it to this day. Recently God began to redirect my life, calling me to crusade evangelism.

He opened the door. I had the right idea. It was just about eighteen years too early—that's all. The Lord led me differently from how I wanted to go. But in his timing he did what I thought he ought to have done a long time ago.

God may lead you differently from how you want to go. He may have put desires in your heart that one day will break ground and bear fruit. But it may be much later. It is during these times of waiting for our fruit to ripen that we must trust him.

God is thinking about you. He is concerned about you. God has a plan and strategy for your life. And what are those thoughts that God is thinking? "I know the thoughts that I think toward you, says the Lord, thoughts of peace and not of evil" (Jeremiah 29:11).

□ □ □ □ □

God may hate sin. But he loves you and me with everlasting love. Even when we fail, he loves us. His thoughts for us ultimately are thoughts of peace. You might say, "But I have failed recently. I have sinned. I have fallen short. What would God say to me?" Jeremiah 3:12 says: " 'Return, backsliding Israel,' says the Lord; 'I will not cause My anger to fall on you. For I am merciful,' says the Lord." God wants you to turn from sin. He wants to bring you into the full relationship he has planned for you.

Remember that the next time Satan whispers in your ear that God's designs for you are evil. Remember this passage and quote it. The next time Satan says God is against you, say, "No, that's not true." Jeremiah 29:11 says: " 'I know the thoughts that I think toward you, says the Lord, thoughts of peace and not of evil, to give you a future and a hope." The next time the devil reminds you of your past, remind him of your future. God has a plan in mind.

Artists hate it when someone offers criticism of a work in progress. A true artist can look at a blank piece of paper, stare at it for a time, and see an idea for a picture begin to emerge. They know what they are going to put on that paper. They view a lump of clay and see a finished product in their mind's eye. Then someone comes along who doesn't have that artistic ability and all they see is a lump of clay. As the artist is forming and working on it, the observer can't see how that glob of clay will ever become a prized work of art.

That's how some people are with God. "Hey, Lord, what are you doing here? What's the plan here? What do you have in mind?" You are a work in progress. You see only the beginning. And the present. God sees the end from the beginning. You see only what is happening now. God sees what he is going to do in the future.

There is a great promise contained in Romans 8:28. It's especially important when we are going through difficulties: "All things work together for good to those who love God, to those who are the called according to His purpose." If life has ever seemed hard and it seems like things are falling apart, here is God's personal pledge and promise. He says, "All things are working together for good." He is in control of all circumstances that surround the life of the Christian. So rejoice! God doesn't make mistakes. He doesn't forget what he is doing.

I am always forgetting things. I start projects, and then I am distracted. My wife does the same thing with cooking. One day she had a steak on the grill. She got on the phone. By the time she got off, the steak was burned to a crisp. I said, "What happened?" She said, "I got on the phone." I'm so glad that when I'm going through a difficult trial, God doesn't get on the phone.

He is mindful of us. He is thinking about us. He never forgets us. Everything that happens in our lives must first come through his protective screen. All things work together.

Notice that verse doesn't say all *good* things work together. It says *all* things—whatever their color, whatever their character. *All* things work together for *good*. David wrote in Psalm 119:91: "For all are Your servants." God is in control.

This does not mean that all things are *good* things. There are things that come in life that are difficult and painful. There are bitter pills to swallow. Things may not be very good for you at this very moment. They may even be painful. But ultimately one day things will work out for *good*.

When God looks at us, he sees the big picture. He is always considering the eternal, while we are considering the temporal. He is always concerned with the spiritual, while we are concerned with the physical.

It's sort of like children. They don't understand when, as a concerned parent, you say, "You need a balanced diet. You can't live on chocolate cake the rest of your life. You can't have Oreos for dinner and ice cream for dessert. You need to eat nutritious food. You have to think about the big picture."

We are usually interested in the short term and things that make us happy—things that make life flow well. When hardship comes, we wonder, *Why is God allowing this?* So we will grow up. So we will learn some lessons. All things are working together.

Sometimes God will interrupt our lives with a detour. I read a story about a woman who was driving home one evening. She noticed that a huge truck was right behind her. In fact, he was right on her bumper. She panicked and stepped on the gas trying to get away from this truck barreling down behind her. Soon they were racing down the freeway. The woman floored it. The truck remained in hot pursuit. Frightened, she pulled off the freeway, and the truck stayed behind her. She panicked. She drove up to a gas station, threw open her car door, and jumped out screaming, "This man is chasing me!" The man in the truck jumped out of the truck, ran over to her, and opened up her rear door. There crouched a rapist who had hidden himself in the backseat of her car. From his vantage point riding higher, the trucker could see the rapist and was chasing her to warn her of the impending danger.

The same is true of God. He sees the dangers that we face from his vantage point. He knows the outcome of each course we have chosen. He tries to warn us—perhaps through our conscience, perhaps through the voice of a friend, perhaps through circumstances. When it seems God is spoiling our fun, he is actually looking out for us: All things are working together for good to those who love God and are called according to his purpose.

□ □ □ □ □

You *can* change directions in life. You *can* receive eternal life. You *can* have complete assurance of that fact. How can you know for sure? Acknowledge that you are a sinner, that regardless of your own standard of "goodness," you can never achieve perfection (which is God's only standard) through your own efforts. Accept that you need forgiveness for your sins. Accept that you cannot achieve God's acceptance through your own good works or personal merit. Accept that you need Jesus, who died on the cross to purchase the complete forgiveness of your sins. His sacrifice paid the price for you. He purchased your entrance into heaven. Ask Jesus to forgive you, as in the suggested prayer at the end of chapter 8.

Once you have asked Christ to forgive you and have invited him into your heart, you have the assurance that you not only have settled the question of eternal life for all time but you have the presence of Christ within you to direct you, protect you, and comfort you for the remainder of your days on earth. Regardless of what you are going through now, Jesus will be with you. He will help you. He will never leave you. He has a perfect plan for your life—a better plan than you could possibly achieve on your own.

Yes, it is true. There is an expected end to your trouble. There is a future for you. There is hope for you. Whatever your circumstances right now, however difficult your situation, there is hope for you. God is thinking about you. His plans for you are good. His future for you is bright. So don't be afraid to offer yourself to him and say, "Lord, I want your will for me."

Now that you have accepted Jesus as Savior, you will want to grow spiritually. Here is a suggested prayer to help you on your way as you learn more about Christ:

Lord, thank you for dying on the cross to pay for my sins. I'm glad that I need not live beneath the weight of guilt and condemnation. Thank you for forgiving me of my sins and giving me a brand-new life. Thank you for the gift of salvation. Thank you for filling me with the Holy Spirit. Lead me in the paths of righteousness. Help me to turn away from the past and to look toward the future with excitement and expectancy. Thank you that your plans for me are good. Teach me your ways. Help me to know you and to serve you consistently. Teach me to pray and read the Bible daily. Help me to understand it and to use it as a road map through life. I pray this in Jesus' name. Amen.

There is a better way to live. It is God's plan for your life. His future for you is better than the future you have planned for yourself. Walk in that plan. Then when this life on earth comes to a close, you will see the Lord face-to-face. To join God in heaven and spend eternity in his presence—that is the answer to your spiritual quest.

NOTES

CHAPTER 1: WHY AM I EMPTY?

1. *USA Today,* 10 April 1991.
2. *GQ,* 1993.
3. John Carlson, Knight-Ridder News Service, April 13, 1994.
4. Ibid.
5. *Rolling Stone,* July 1995.
6. John Carlson, Knight-Ridder News Service, 13 April 1994.
7. *Us,* June 1990.
8. *People* (no date).
9. *People,* 28 May 1998.
10. *Entertainment Weekly,* 23 June 2000.
11. Loomis Cage, *Stars and Bars—Part II,* chapter 6, 1984.

CHAPTER 2: WHY AM I LONELY?

1. *USA Today,* 17 April 1992.

CHAPTER 3: WHY AM I AFRAID?

1. The term *rapture,* while not found in the Bible, is used to describe an event widely accepted as the moment when Jesus wll gather all true believers into heaven with him (see 1 Thessalonians 4:17).

CHAPTER 4: WHY AM I HERE?

1. Wade Clark Roof, *A Generation of Seekers* (San Francisco: HarperSanFrancisco, 1993).
2. Greg Laurie, *The Great Compromise,* (Dallas: Word Publishing, 1994).

CHAPTER 5: WHAT HAPPENS WHEN I DIE?

1. *Us,* 1995.
2. *People,* 28 May 2000.

CHAPTER 7: WHY DO I FEEL GUILTY?

1. John MacArthur, *The Vanishing Conscience* (Dallas: Word Publishing, 1994).
2. Ibid.
3. Ibid.
4. Ibid.
5. Ibid.
6. Charles Sikes, *A Nation of Victims* (New York: St. Martins Press, 1992).

NOTE TO THE READER:
THE NEXT STEP

If you have made a personal commitment to follow Jesus Christ, please write me. I would love to hear from you!

Greg Laurie
Harvest Ministries
P.O. Box 4424
Riverside, CA 92504

You can also check out our Web site at www.harvest.org. There you will find many helpful resources to help you grow spiritually. I also want to recommend a Bible that has been custom designed for a person just like you. It's called *The New Believer's Bible*. Written in the very understandable New Living Translation, it takes you step-by-step through the basics of growing in your newfound faith and contains hundreds of notes that deal with everything from studies on God, angels, and Satan to how to pray effectively, how to know God's will, how to resist temptation, and much more.

If you have not yet made a commitment to Christ, let me encourage you to get a copy of *The Seeker's Bible* (New Testament). It is written for a person who is looking for the truth but has not made a personal commitment to Christ.

God bless you.
Greg Laurie

ABOUT THE AUTHOR

Greg Laurie is senior pastor of Harvest Christian Fellowship in Riverside, California, and the host of *A New Beginning* radio and television program. He is the featured evangelist for Harvest Crusades, a contemporary outreach that has touched over one million lives with the gospel of Jesus Christ. He is the author of six books and is the general editor of *The New Believer's Bible.* Greg lives with his wife and two sons in southern California.

Steps to Peace with God

 Step 1 God's Purpose:
Peace and Life

God loves you and wants you to experience peace and life—abundant and eternal.

The Bible Says . . .

". . . we have peace with God through our Lord Jesus Christ." Romans 5:1

"For God so loved the world that He gave His only begotten Son, that whoever believes in Him should not perish but have everlasting life." John 3:16

". . . I have come that they may have life, and that they may have it more abundantly." John 10:10b

Since God planned for us to have peace and the abundant life right now, why are most people not having this experience?

 Step 2 Our Problem:
Separation

God created us in His own image to have an abundant life. He did not make us as robots to automatically love and obey Him, but gave us a will and a freedom of choice.

We chose to disobey God and go our own willful way. We still make this choice today. This results in separation from God.

Our choice results in separation from God.

The Bible Says . . .

"For all have sinned and fall short of the glory of God." Romans 3:23

"For the wages of sin is death, but the gift of God is eternal life in Christ Jesus our Lord." Romans 6:23

People (Sinful)   God (Holy)

Our Attempts

Through the ages, individuals have tried in many ways to bridge this gap . . . without success . . .

There is only one remedy for this problem of separation.

The Bible Says . . .

"There is a way that seems right to man, but in the end it leads to death." Proverbs 14:12

"But your iniquities have separated you from God; and your sins have hidden His face from you, so that He will not hear." Isaiah 59:2

Step 3 God's Remedy: The Cross

Jesus Christ is the only answer to this problem. He died on the Cross and rose from the grave, paying the penalty for our sin and bridging the gap between God and people.

The Bible Says . . .

". . . God is on one side and all the people on the other side, and Christ Jesus, Himself man, is between them to bring them together . . ." 1 Timothy 2:5

"For Christ also has suffered once for sins, the just for the unjust, that He might bring us to God . . ." 1 Peter 3:18a

"But God demonstrates His own love for us in this: While we were still sinners, Christ died for us." Romans 5:8

God has provided the only way . . . we must make the choice . . .

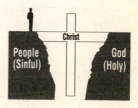

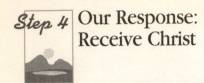

Step 4 Our Response: Receive Christ

We must trust Jesus Christ and receive Him by personal invitation.

The Bible Says . . .

"Behold, I stand at the door and knock. If anyone hears My voice and opens the door, I will come in to him and dine with him, and he with Me." Revelation 3:20

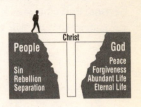

Are you here . . . or here?

"But as many as received Him, to them He gave the right to become children of God, even to those who believe in His name." John 1:12

". . . if you confess with your mouth the Lord Jesus and believe in your heart that God has raised Him from the dead, you will be saved." Romans 10:9

Is there any good reason why you cannot receive Jesus Christ right now?

How to receive Christ:

1. Admit your need (I am a sinner).
2. Be willing to turn from your sins (repent).
3. Believe that Jesus Christ died for you on the Cross and rose from the grave.
4. Through prayer, invite Jesus Christ to come in and control your life through the Holy Spirit. (Receive Him as Lord and Savior.)

What to Pray:

Dear Lord Jesus,
    I know that I am a sinner and need Your forgiveness. I believe that You died for my sins. I want to turn from my sins. I now invite You to come into my heart and life. I want to trust and follow You as Lord and Savior.

In Jesus' name. Amen.

_____   _____
        Date   Signature

God's Assurance: His Word

If you prayed this prayer,

The Bible Says...

"For 'whoever calls upon the name of the Lord will be saved.'" Romans 10:13

Did you sincerely ask Jesus Christ to come into your life? Where is He right now? What has He given you?

"For it is by grace you have been saved, through faith—and this is not from yourselves, it is the gift of God—not by works, so that no one can boast." Ephesians 2:8,9

The Bible Says...

"He who has the Son has life; he who does not have the Son of God does not have life. These things I have written to you who believe in the name of the Son of God, that you may know that you have eternal life, and that you may continue to believe in the name of the Son of God." 1 John 5:12–13, NKJV

Receiving Christ, we are born into God's family through the supernatural work of the Holy Spirit who indwells every believer...this is called regeneration or the "new birth."

This is just the beginning of a wonderful new life in Christ. To deepen this relationship you should:

1. Read your Bible every day to know Christ better.
2. Talk to God in prayer every day.
3. Tell others about Christ.
4. Worship, fellowship, and serve with other Christians in a church where Christ is preached.
5. As Christ's representative in a needy world, demonstrate your new life by your love and concern for others.

God bless you as you do.

Billy Graham

If you want further help in the decision you have made, write to:
Billy Graham Evangelistic Association P.O. Box 779, Minneapolis, Minnesota 55440-0779

If you are committing your life to Christ, please let us know! We would like to send you Bible study materials and a complimentary six-month subscription to *Decision* magazine to help you grow in your faith.

The Billy Graham Evangelistic Association exists to support the evangelistic ministry and calling of Billy Graham to take the message of Christ to all we can by every prudent means available to us.

Our desire is to introduce as many as we can to the person of Jesus Christ, so that they might experience His love and forgiveness.

Your prayers are the most important way to support us in this ministry. We are grateful for the dedicated prayer support we receive. We are also grateful for those that support us with contributions.

Giving can be a rewarding experience for you and for us at the Billy Graham Evangelistic Association (BGEA). Your gift gives you the satisfaction of supporting an organization that is actively involved in evangelism. Also, it is encouraging to us because part of our ministry is devoted to helping people like you discover and enjoy the stewardship of giving wisely and effectively.

Billy Graham Evangelistic Association
P.O. Box 779
Minneapolis, Minnesota 55440-0779
www.billygraham.org

Billy Graham Evangelistic Association of Canada
P.O. Box 841, Stn Main
Winnipeg, Manitoba R3C 2R3
www.billygraham.ca

Toll free: 1-877-247-2426